CW00330562

About the Author

Adam Hayes lives independently in his flat on the coast of West Sussex. He employs his own personal assistants. He has played the disability sport boccia to international level, and wheelchair football for Brighton and Hove Albion. Adam is a qualified sports coach and offers voluntary coaching services. He broadcasts four hours a week on a London internet radio station which streams worldwide. He gives talks on Disability and Independence to schoolchildren. He hopes in the future to gain suitable qualifications so that he can offer professional support to people seeking an independent life. This is his first book, which he hopes you will enjoy.

Thirty Years of Me

Adam Hayes

Thirty Years of Me

Olympia Publishers
London

www.olympiapublishers.com
OLYMPIA PAPERBACK EDITION

Copyright © Adam Hayes 2022

The right of Adam Hayes to be identified as author of
this work has been asserted in accordance with sections 77 and 78 of
the Copyright, Designs and Patents Act 1988.

All Rights Reserved

No reproduction, copy or transmission of this publication
may be made without written permission.
No paragraph of this publication may be reproduced,
copied or transmitted save with the written permission of the publisher,
or in accordance with the provisions
of the Copyright Act 1956 (as amended).

Any person who commits any unauthorised act in relation to
this publication may be liable to criminal
prosecution and civil claims for damage.

A CIP catalogue record for this title is
available from the British Library.

ISBN: 978-1-80074-627-5

The author believes all the events in this book are true. Conversations
are inevitably approximations, the best that can be recalled. The author
is solely responsible for the accuracy of this account of his life and he
welcomes any comments from readers via the publisher.

First Published in 2022

Olympia Publishers
Tallis House
2 Tallis Street
London
EC4Y 0AB

Printed in Great Britain

Dedication

I would like to dedicate this book to all the people who have
supported me during my first 30 years.

Acknowledgements

I would like to give sincere thanks to my scribe, Mr Gardner, for his dedication and commitment throughout the year of writing the book.

Chapter One

Enabling Me

My unique introduction to the world

I would like to explain to you my start in life. It was not run-of-the-mill! I was born at the Royal Sussex Hospital in Brighton, weighing just a bag of sugar: two pounds. I was what is commonly known as a premature baby. I was also delivered via a caesarean operation, so from what I am led to believe there were many complications on my entry into the world. It wasn't just complicated, but also dangerous for both my mum and I, so much so that they had to rush my unconscious mum into labour to deliver me in the safest way possible. I wasn't born in Worthing Hospital, my local, because they didn't have the expertise to give my mum the vital treatment that she needed at such a critical time. That was why she was rushed by ambulance along the coast road to meet specialists waiting for her at A & E. During this critical time, we were both fighting for our lives. To all who were involved in saving our lives, from the emergency services to the specialist doctors and nurses, great thanks!

Once I was stable, I was placed in an incubator for several months. My first experience of an operating theatre I can only imagine, because I was only months old. However, I have been told I had a hernia operation which thankfully was another success. During my period at the Royal Sussex Hospital, specialists began to notice that my physical condition was a bit different from what they were familiar with. In other words, I wasn't doing what other babies were doing, for example moving my legs and arms. It was soon after this that the doctors gave my family the diagnosis. I had cerebral palsy (CP). Obviously, I cannot tell you my family's immediate response. It must have been a great shock. On the other hand, immediately it was a mission they all were dedicated to fulfil.

Following the most current wisdom on CP, I was seen by various surgeons to see how they could improve my body. They started with an operation to loosen my groin muscles. This had to be done on more than one occasion, and it extended my stay in hospital. After a period of recovery, it was time for me to experience the outside world for the very first time since entering it in my unique way!

The hospital visits didn't stop there. As I was growing, my mum noticed I was crying more than normal. She took me to the doctors. He made me an appointment to have an x-ray to get to the bottom of it. It revealed my hips were out of joint, and the only way to relieve the pain was to operate. When I was in theatre, surgeons realised my left hip was indeed badly dislocated. To put this right they had to insert a metal plate with several screws to keep my hip aligned. Thankfully, the lead surgeon, Mr Clark, did a remarkable job. But I was in plaster of Paris with a bar in between my legs to keep them apart for six to eight weeks.

My family quickly began to realise what life was going to be like, certainly during my early years anyway. As you can imagine, this put a lot of pressure on my mum and family during this time. So, thank you for everything. I really can't say for sure how they feel, but what I can tell you is if it wasn't for the family sticking together, I wouldn't be here writing this book.

As I grew through two, three, and then four years old, more surgery was to follow. This time it was to loosen the tendons in my groin on the advice of physiotherapists and consultants. The operations were successful and, as the weeks and months passed, the family and the specialists began to notice steady improvements with how I was moving my legs. That was great news and a relief to my family. I was given regular physiotherapy to improve things further. After several months of physiotherapy, my hamstrings became, for some reason, incredibly tight, so I had to go back into hospital to have these loosened before the tightness became irreversible.

I was already known as the miracle baby. This was because, when I was a few hours old, my heart stopped beating. It was only with the last compressions that they managed to bring me back to life. This is the right time to give you my opinion of why I have cerebral palsy. Due to the period when they had to bring me back to life, all this time my body wasn't getting the oxygen needed to vital organs so, in layman's terms, this caused my lack of movement. The part of the brain which is damaged is called the cerebellum. It is the area of the brain that controls our movements and co-ordination. Please bear in mind, what I have written is what I understand about my own disability. I can't speak for anyone else's circumstances.

You may be wondering when I started to become aware of what was going on and how severe it was. Well, I can tell you that my earliest memories come from when I had my groin and hips operated on. That was when I was five. The reason I can remember this is because, yet again, I was being put into plaster of Paris with the divide bar to separate my legs and the excruciating pain that came along with it. It is fair to say I had a good set of lungs! When I arrived home from hospital, the kitchen became my bedroom because my brothers were unable to carry me upstairs, for obvious reasons. I am sure this was yet another emotional and challenging time for my family. Being a kid, I took it all in my young stride, but now I am older all I can say is what a bloody drama! My thought processes at this point were still immature, so it didn't really occur to me that there was much wrong with my situation. I just thought that it was the norm, and that this is what happened when everyone comes into the world. It wasn't until I hit seven or eight years of age that I realised what an emotional journey my family had been on, all those years before. I don't even have the words to describe what they must have felt, apart from: WHY US?

I am absolutely certain that it was the support from my nan and grandad that provided the vital strength that allowed my mum to get through all the challenges and hurdles during my young, traumatic start in life. Bear in mind, of my three siblings she was still bringing up two of them besides myself (Darren, the oldest, by this time was 18 years old and was starting to go his own way). However, even with my nan and grandad's support, this was a hell of a lot of pressure for one parent to cope with, as I am sure a lot of parents reading this book will appreciate!

Some of you might be wondering where my second parent was in all of this. He didn't like it when things got tough so, instead of confronting it like the rest of us, his way of dealing with it was to run off, not sparing a thought for anyone else but himself and his own emotions. All I can say of this part is that he sure has missed out on a heck of a lot. Mick/Dad, if you're reading this, I guess lesson learnt. STOP RUNNING! I hope you are proud of yourself.

During these hard times, unfortunately, my second so-called

parent, aka Dad, only wanted to be involved when things were looking up, especially when the idea was put to me that I should start doing karate to build my muscles and support my development. Mick was a karate instructor. He jumped at the chance to get me involved in karate, so sure enough I was the first kid with a disability that I know of competing in karate with the help of the instructors, my mum, and Mick – however, that was only when it suited him, to make him look good in front of his colleagues. In my opinion, this is no way to behave as a parent, so to all you young gentlemen: do not take a leaf out of Mick's book. Always be there for your wife, daughter, or son, whatever the circumstances, good or bad. Your children only get one birth family!

Growing up from age five

From age five, I soon realised in my own way what kind of family I was born into. Regardless of my disability, my family have taught and encouraged me always to sit on my own two bum cheeks. You don't get things in life for free. You have to work for what you want and deserve.

That being said, I was a very inquisitive and interested child. I would always see what different objects I could pick up independently and came to realise that not everything is possible without adaptations. For example, I tried picking up my own CDs, fell over the top of my arm rest while doing so and landed on the floor.

"What the hell are you doing down there?" said Mum.

"I am trying to do things for myself!"

After being picked up off the floor with a few bruises, my mum taught me another way of being independent – use your brain! Independence isn't only using your body. Become mentally independent and be more realistic as to what can be done physically for yourself. I learned the dos and the don'ts of having a disability. Where there's a wheel, there's a way.

There was much more for me to figure out …and that came about with the arrival of SCHOOL.

When I began school, I felt very ostracised to start with, but, bearing in mind what my family had taught me, I was determined that I would fit in, regardless of disability, shape, size, or colour. It was all down to whether I allowed myself to take one more gigantic step. I remember those days more vividly than recent ones, because I was experiencing things that other children would not. There were more surprises and even shocks ahead of me.

Chapter Two

Mainstream

Pushing the boundaries at primary school

The biggest shock was seeing people's reactions towards me. The majority were positive, but there was negativity too. An example of a positive reaction was that no matter what class I was put in, the students in that particular class treated me as an individual and seemed blind to the fact that I had a disability. A negative example was that I was frequently reminded of my disability when my peers were playing sport. This is because the teachers told me it would be too dangerous for me to play sport, as I may cause an accident or run into someone in my wheelchair by accident. However, I knew this not to be true, as I had taken up karate on weeknights after school and during the occasional weekend. I could do all that and not cause an accident. My family were also taking karate lessons, encouraged by my dad who was actually a karate instructor. Nobody got hurt!

You can understand that the school's policies on health and safety rules were making me feel very isolated. I wasn't able to do what I knew I could do because of rules and regulations. At this point, let me give you a little secret: *it was the world that was disabling me, not my body.*

That became obvious by Year 6, when my class had a lesson upstairs. Disability and stairs do not mix. I had to endure not being able to be involved with all my peers. I was set a different task from them, which made me feel different, inside and out. Over time, I began to accept that sometimes things are just not possible unless you have the attitude to change it. I suggested to my form tutor to adapt where the lessons took place. Rather than the lessons taking place upstairs, my suggestion was to bring the lessons to me downstairs.

As soon as I said this, my tutor, Mr Pearson, looked at me rather bemused and said, "I will trial it for a month and see how we go."

"Thank you, Mr Pearson, for allowing me a trial, and experience the wonderful world of change!"

Mr Pearson made the change possible. I began to get the bug. I began to gain confidence. I went to my headteacher, Mr Hoffton, and discussed the possibility of me joining in sport with the rest of my form. We agreed that if I had a member of staff to observe safety, I was OK to join in, but ONLY with my LSA (Learning Support Assistant) present. That concession gave me a great sense of achievement and pride at such a young age. It taught me a valuable lesson: *I could take on the world providing I had a plan*. Is this not normal behaviour for the average Year 6 pupil? The good thing about having a disability is the that you have to have a plan for many things, if you want to avoid any mishaps.

Of course, it didn't always work out, particularly if you decided to be a bit spontaneous, as I frequently have been known to be, ditching the plan and pushing back boundaries. I once crossed the field at playtime to play football **without an LSA**. I chose to adapt how I was able to play by going in goal so peers could try and score past me. One of my peers took a shot which I saved – but there was a consequence, and that consequence was a numb face! This is what happens when you go against rules set by headteachers.

I suppose you could say that learning from your impulses is a key part of growing up. Whilst on the subject of growing up, it was nearly time for a big change. Change is something of a taboo subject for most of the population, including me. Not knowing what was ahead of me, when all my other peers already knew the senior schools that they would be transferring to, was quite a daunting prospect. I was about to enter unknown territory, after having been so comfortable in my surroundings for many years. However, I did have approximately six weeks to get used to the fact my life was about to change dramatically. For some strange reason, I didn't know what the changes were going to consist of, so I had to keep an open mind. When I rolled out of my mainstream school for the very last time and was assisted into my taxi, the one that I got each and every day to and from school, it came with a feeling of numbness and confusion for the whole journey home. I was trying to get my head around what was about to occur.

I was approaching the council estate I used to live on. This made me feel very strange, as I knew this would be the last ever time I would be in my taxi on this particular route to mainstream primary school. It was an incredibly emotional moment. I took my time in reversing onto the ramp to get out of the vehicle. I found this particular situation very challenging, hard to come to terms with. In other words, you could cut my feelings with a knife. Once off the ramps, I span round and I immediately felt my emotions disappear like water off a duck's back. I was in familiar surroundings once again. It was time for the six weeks holiday to begin, when I would get up to all my old antics like any other kid. One of my antics consisted of pulling my friends around on Tesco shopping carts while they were holding onto the back of my chair, thinking I was Michael Schumacher. I knew that I had something in common with Michael: we were both legends, as I felt I was the king of my kingdom. Feeling I was a king enabled me to feel in control of my own destiny. Making up my own rules. Disobeying my mum when she told me to come in for my fish fingers, chips, and beans. After all, I was not Tony Blair, thinking I could turn up to Parliament in my pyjamas while eating strawberry scones. I'll let you know these were not just scones, they were Parliamentary scones. This is the same as saying that I was just a kid.

The end of the six-week holiday was fast approaching, so I knew it was time to get serious and start thinking about THE FUTURE! The next morning, as a family, we had a big occasion, almost as big as the Queen's Speech. We were meeting with a social worker about what would happen next. This was to determine where my secondary education would take place. It was a particularly difficult time for all of us, because my parents believed that they knew what was best for me (this was the last time up to this present day that my dad was involved in my life).

We had to give proof to the authorities and the people with the moneybags and purse strings about why what we had in mind was the right avenue for my future. Like everything, all a local authority sees is pound signs, not the individual's needs.

Following this meeting, my future had to be decided at a tribunal. A tribunal is a posh word for posh people having a dispute about a particular situation that has to be settled. My tribunal was to decide whether mainstream education or specialist school education, with all the therapies that I would need to help develop my independence and life skills, was the right decision. The authority's preferred outcome was for me to attend my local mainstream secondary school, knowing that it had a specialist unit for disabled students. The social worker did not realise that my mum had previously visited the school, and she knew Angmering School wasn't the right place for my development, as they did not offer the services required for my level of disability. Given the circumstances, a dispute was bound to happen, whether we wanted it or not. The most important stage of my life so far was on the line. Given this choice between mainstream school and specialist school, my social worker at the time put a very generous suggestion of an alternative placement to my parents, and his suggestion was Lord Mayor Treloar School. Eventually after all the hoo-haa and toing and froing over cutting costs, it was decided and agreed by all concerned that Treloar, although much more expensive, was to be my next place of education, much to everyone's relief.

Visiting Treloar School

Once all was agreed it was now time to prepare for the next chapter of my life. The first part thing to do was to gather my thoughts. What lay ahead for me in the coming months and year? How would I know how to handle situations, and my feelings, in a positive way? I tried to control an overwhelming feeling of nervous energy. Given the prospect that I was about to leave my family for the very first time in my life and go to unfamiliar surroundings – a boarding school that was approximately an hour and a half commute by car from home - it was a very alien idea for me.

"Who on earth thought of this! Oh, I know, the wonderful people called social workers!"

I therefore decided to go along with their incredibly long-distance alien plan and decided to take a look at the place with my own eyes and bum cheeks. So off I went to look at my very own Hogwarts! As we approached the Treloar front door, I shared the analogy with my mum.

"I didn't know you wanted me to take flying lessons on a broomstick! You could have just said you wanted me to be the next Daniel Radcliffe instead of dragging me to this strange gaffe. What the hell!"

Anyway, in we went.

When those huge electric doors opened in front of me for the first time, I realised that what I had imagined was not indeed the reality. What do I mean by this? I felt able-bodied (!), that's what I mean. I could control my muscle movements to a reasonable degree. I was going past people whose bodies were completely out of control.

"Look at the way that boy's moving! I can learn acrobatics! Cheers, Mum."

"Do not be so disrespectful and lippy!" said Mum. "I did not bring you up to be like this!"

Whilst we were continuing our what seemed like never-ending tour, I came across a talking computer.

"It's like a walking, talking Stephen Hawking. This place is freaky but amazing! A bit like us."

"Speak for yourself!".

"No, Mum, you didn't bring me up to be selfish. I mean, I would feel bad if I didn't include you."

On we went down the fifty thousandth corridor, only to find the best thing known to the world: food. Approaching the canteen, in front of my eyes I saw what I described at the time as a lazy person's best friend: an automatic spoon. It's what's called a neater eater, which is something that assists someone struggling to move their limbs to eat their food independently.

"What's on the menu?"

I was handed a menu to look at.

"Mum, this food looks fit for a king."

However, my taste buds told me a different story. Needless to say, the food wasn't great, but beggars can't be choosers, so I just cracked on. Whilst eating, one of the current students came to the table. At age twelve years, apart from myself and another family member, I had never met another disabled person before, so naturally I thought we were the only disabled people in the UK. When this student approached my table, my reaction to my mum was:

"I think that guy needs a tissue."

You see, I did not realise dribbling was one of the factors of his condition. It sounds so weird saying that, knowing what I know now.

"Don't be so disrespectful. It's not his fault."

"Chill out! I didn't know that."

After lunch, the visit continued on to where I would reside if I became a student, which was looking increasingly inevitable. I saw the boarding house for the first time

"I'm not staying in this! I want to achieve the maximum, not the minimum."

The reason for this response was that I thought I would go backwards not forwards, seeing all the mobility aids that were in front of me. I wasn't sure what they all were, due to my lack of understanding and very limited knowledge of disability. I was naturally freaked out, as you can imagine. My mum sat down with me and explained.

"You know, when you were younger you wanted to do as much as you could for yourself. These contraptions will be able to support you in doing those things that you wanted to do without falling over your arm-rest."

I thought about this.

23

"If I come here and then come home at the end of the week on a Friday don't expect me to look like the same person. Expect me to look like ET!"

The reason for my ET analogy was because a lot of people in society look to ET as a creature who is both different and experimental. This is exactly how I felt about the situation in front of me: different and experimental. I felt like I was in a movie alongside ET, because of the amount of difference and experimenting that was going on both physically and mentally. I was trying to get used to my mum's explanation in my own way. And my conclusion was that all these new experiences made me feel like I was having an out of body experience. I just didn't know what was what and who was who. However, this was my chance to crack change, and turn this from an out of body experience into a reality. That being said, I was still scared at how much or how little would change. But it didn't stop me from taking that step and giving things a go.

Before going home from the visit, I wanted to have the chance at giving the contraptions a try. So, I did. I dropped my phone, grabbed a contraption otherwise known as a grabber, squeezed the grabber handle which then resulted in me being able to pick the phone up off the floor without nose-diving over my arm rest, which I thought was amazing.

"Challenge accepted. Not that scary after all. When do I start?"

It was the end of the visit and time to go home. During the journey home I tried to digest all of the freaky experiences I had had, whilst at the same time listening to my euphoric music. Then back into Adam's World.

Chapter Three

Difference

Leaving home to be a weekly boarder

Before I knew it, I was home, seeing my neighbours walking around the street in their hair curlers and dressing gowns with fags hanging out of their mouths.

"Safe again. Eating my fish fingers, chips, and beans and watching a bit of *Eastenders*."

One weekend, someone told me to do something out of the familiar routine. By this I mean it wasn't the norm. I had to go out for the day in my wheelchair with my friends, only to return to a load of people outside my house saying "SURPRISE!" My family had only gone and organised a leaving home party!

"Oh, by the way, your place at Treloar has been accepted and you start next week."

Shock! I'm leaving my comfort zone for weeks on end!

Sure enough, the Sunday came around quickly, so it was time for me to pack my belongings and take off to Treloar School. My transport arrived to begin my new adventure. I remember the exact feeling. Getting into the transport felt like getting into a sweat box to go to prison. To make the journey bearable, I asked the taxi driver to take my case of CDs and put *Trance Classics 2000* on for the journey.

Little did I know, we had other students to pick up. When

we were approaching the first pick up, I felt a degree of discomfort as I didn't know what to expect, or indeed what their reaction would be towards ET (aka myself). When the back doors opened and the student drove her chair up alongside mine, I relaxed because I could see there was an instant connection. I had realised instantaneously that I was going to be able to support people who had higher levels of need than myself. By higher levels of need, I mean in this case that my fellow traveller had a problem communicating by word of mouth. In fact, it was almost like tuning in to a radio station that you could not quite get reception for. The way she was able to speak, it was hard for me to understand. Advice time: Always Give People The Chance To Use One Of Our most Basic and Free Toolboxes – i.e. TO COMMUNICATE. No matter how long it takes, it's about persisting until you get the right strategies that work for both of you. Don't be scared or think you are being rude when you don't understand them, and get them to repeat as many times as they and you need. They really want to communicate verbally with you.

On we went to Chichester for the next person to pick up and towards the start of my new adventure. The first pick up had been a new experience. It had changed me, my feelings, my emotions somewhat. I felt that I had smoothly overcome my first big challenge, and that the worst was over, because I had never in my life met someone I had to tune in for. On our arrival at the Chichester pick up, I met a new lad joining us in the sweat box. Once he was on board it was time to head towards our final destination, Treloar School, aka Hogwarts.

On this last leg of the journey, I was hilariously informed by the student next to me that I had fallen asleep with my mouth wide open looking like I was catching flies. All I remember was it going extremely quiet, only to be woken up by the silence when the engine was turned off. I was disorientated. Where were we?

"Oh, we have arrived."

Still half asleep, I had to reverse my lovely chariot onto the sweat box ramp. I took a massively deep breath.

"Let the fun and experiment begin!"

Settling in to Treloar School

When approaching Maple House, where I would be boarding, I was greeted by my unit leader. She was what I would call everyone's great nan. She made me feel at ease almost immediately. Because of her, I felt that I could be more like myself and continue where I left off at home. She helped me unpack my stuff and I started to settle in.

The first thing I remember her unpacking was my favourite bit of equipment, my CD player with an assortment of CDs. After putting clothes in the wardrobe and drawers, I asked politely to be left to my own devices for a period of time. Now I was on my own, I had to make it clear to other students that, just because I was at a new place, I was not about to change my characteristics and go quiet and withdrawn. I have always been an extrovert. Just as if I was at home, I turned my music up loud so the rest of my unit could hear me. After all, several staff had advised me to treat this as my home, so I took this literally.

After a while I got bored with my music. I wanted to explore. I could hear other students banging and crashing about.

"What on God's Earth is all this commotion?"

I turned the corner to find four students playing wheelchair hockey. I was intrigued.

"Let me join in please!"

27

"Hi, who are you?"

"Adam."

"Hello, mate. Welcome."

From that moment on, I immediately knew these kids were on my level, so I began playing wheelchair hockey. That meant teaching myself how to adapt things – by myself, without a therapist or specialist in sight. I started straightaway, and grabbed the gaffer tape, then stuck the gaffer tape round the stick as well as the chair to hold the stick in position so I could play the game. This enabled me to play this new sport completely independently, without getting told that I couldn't do something due to safety reasons and red tape (only gaffer tape!) And the rest is history.

After my frantic revelations on the hockey pitch, it was time for glorious, glorious food. Off we all wheeled, sticks and all, to the canteen, where me and the four other lads sat on the same table together from then until Year 9 when we all changed boarding houses. My first ever dinner was chili con carne with rice and, for pud, Red Leicester cheese and crackers.

During our fantastic meal, this rather scary looking man came up me.

"Hi, I'm your manager, John. Nice to meet you."

"Hi, fellah, how're you doing? I'm loving your beard. What shampoo do you use? Head and Shoulders, I'm assuming."

This was the first of many encounters. As the evening went forward, I quickly realised some of the rules, not to be broken. I decided not to go back to the boarding house, but to continue playing hockey until John the manager came into the hall.

"Lads, you do realise it's nine o'clock in the evening. You are meant to be in the boarding house by eight!"

"Don't look at me. I am new," I replied.

As we went off to our rooms, the other lads apologised.

"Sorry. We forgot to tell you that bit."

I realised they liked to push boundaries the same as I did. I also remember John's final words before I went to sleep.

"You will learn very quickly in this place, my son."

The night went on and dawn drew closer, when I was suddenly woken up by this animal-sounding noise.

"What on earth...!"

The noise came and went and came again. Another one of those experiences that were unfamiliar and hard to comprehend! I had never met anything like this in my life.

Anyway, in the morning the staff members were very pleasant and introduced themselves and, while I was being helped to get dressed, I felt very able to say how I felt when they asked me how my first night had gone. I told them it had been a bit strange, especially when I heard what sounded like a wolf howl. They smiled.

"Ah, why don't you come and meet the student responsible for the wolf howl."

"Er, well...OK."

Another challenge. I decided to meet it head on.

"OK...you first!"

So, in we went.

"Adam, this is your room-mate."

I replied in a bubbly manner.

"Oh, nice to meet you, mate. How's it going?"

I was expecting a reply but it wasn't forthcoming. This actually took me back to my journey at the start of the term – on the minibus with the girl with communication issues – so I thought to myself that he must be able to communicate some way; I just had to figure out how. I later learnt his communication was all done with eye movement and an alphabet chart. His eventual response arrived.

"Hi, nice to meet you too."

While this process with the eye movement and communication aid was taking place, I felt astonished. Never in my life had I any idea that there were so many different levels of need. I learnt more than the average Joe in the first 48 hours of my new adventure.

Why Mum chose Treloar School

Interestingly, my mum had been telling me she was sending me to Treloar not to develop my independence but because of my behaviour. I now know as a mature young man that in my mum's mind it was to promote my maximum independence, but that is not what she told me at the time. Growing up with a disability, I didn't think anything of it. But she was right. I had been pushing all sorts of boundaries and limits to the full like any other kid. This had consequences and led to me making mistakes. For sure, my mum always threatened the possibility of boarding school. Me being me, I didn't take a blind bit of notice and carried on pushing these boundaries and limits, until my mum got to the end of her tether and off to boarding school I went.

Maybe it was the following event that made her realise that the time had come to go to boarding school.

One day, I needed no persuading by one of my friends on the estate.

"Adam, why don't we go to the Lamb Park to play some football?"

"Why not! Let's go!"

During this particular gallivanting experience, I was wheeling over the green when, all of a sudden, I heard a pop. I looked down the side of my wheelchair only to find my castor wheel had sheered and fallen off. It reminded me of *Only Fools and Horses,* as I only had three wheels like their Robin Reliant.

Unbeknown to me, my big brother Darren, aka Lurch, was out in his Ford Transit van looking for me. When he found me, I was travelling home with one of my friends on the back of my chair to keep the balance. My brother flashed his headlights at me, and stuck his head out the window.

"Stop there, you little git!"

He jumped out of the van and assessed the situation.

"I think we need reinforcements. It is not safe for you to go home on three wheels."

After several phone calls, four friendly giants appeared to assist my brother to get my Storm 3 twenty-four-volt-powered wheelchair into the back of his van, whilst I was tossed onto the front seat and belted up.

So, when my mother agreed to my going away to boarding school, I believed this was a result of my behaviour and incidents such as this one. But indeed, this wasn't the case, as I found out several years later. My mum had my best interests at heart. I would like personally to say thank you, Mum. If it wasn't for my new Treloar adventure, I wouldn't have learnt as much as I did in those first forty-eight hours.

Chapter Four

Limitless

Learning more control

Mr First Week. I began to feel like the most popular student in the world as every therapist wanted a limb! Or rather, to see me at the same time. This was due to the number of assessments needed to build my care plan for the rest of my Hogwarts experience.

After this week of demanding assessments, it was time to return home to my family on the Friday for the weekend. When I arrived back home, my mum could not believe the transformation both physically and mentally. I was finally able to practise my new skills, as I was creating a plan to do things independently during those therapy assessments.

Here is an example: I could, for the first time, pick up CDs without dropping them every five seconds, simply by practising what I had learnt. It was all to do with controlling my body movements through breathing and positioning my body and chair according to the task I was carrying out. Contrast that with the way I used to do things: everything would be rushed, my body would then tense up and that caused my muscles to contract to such an extent I did not have the strength or dexterity in my fingers to keep a grip on things. Over my first week at Treloar, through my various assessments, this situation rapidly and consistently changed, which came as something of a surprise even to myself. Who would have thought a simple positional change of my wheelchair would be the answer to giving me better control and movement on the stronger side of my body?

I would like to guide you in making these changes by describing a specific scenario.

Picking up a pen that is lying on a table

Step 1: Make sure your body is at the most comfortable point for you. Take some deep breaths until you feel your muscles are relaxed enough for your body to pick up the pen.

Step 2: Approach the surface on which the pen lies. It is vitally important to be head-on, so your knees go under the table while making sure you have a bird's eye view.

Step 3: If you have a tilt and recline function on your chair, make sure you use it to give you maximum potential to achieve the task.

Step 4: Once your position is all set and you are comfortable, take some more deep breaths to further relax your body and make sure your hand is in a claw-like position, if achievable, over the object you're trying to pick up. This is to gain maximum control when carrying out the task – in this case, picking up a pen. Please bear in mind that this was a personal task set by Occupational therapists (OTs) specifically designed for my need, so it may not work for everyone. This proves there is more than one way to skin a cat. By all means give it a whirl.

You can imagine that this was a very strange development for my family, as I imagine it was like having a new son and brother in the family. Because of my new and improved physicality, I started to do things that had been previously unheard of, and almost impossible from the family's point of view. It almost felt like I was as free as a bird flying in the sky. I was at long last able to, and quietly confident to, carry out tasks and challenges knowing I was safe to do so because I had a pre-plan to stick to, set by the OTs at Treloar. This meant I was not having to ask my mum if it was OK to do things because of my safety. I would now just crack on with the plan in place. For my family, I'm sure this was like a weight being lifted, seeing my newfound independence. I always knew in the back of my mind that my family would be very apprehensive and nervous, given that they hadn't seen anything like this in me before. Any concerns they had were completely understandable. I just told them to 'please trust me' and that 'I have been in magical hands for the past week'. Those hands 'had my best interests at heart', so all the work they would be doing would have a positive outcome for all of us.

"So, why not?"

Trust

After being home for the weekend, I returned to Treloar with a great sense of relief, because I knew Treloar had already found trust in me. Therefore, I continued to thrive under the tutelage of all involved. I was able to concentrate solely on thriving, rather than worrying about building blocks of trust with my family. Building blocks became a common theme each time I returned home, as I would try to instil the same level of confidence into my family that Treloar had in me, so they would both be singing from the same hymn sheet. So, you can understand what I mean when I say this was very much the same as building a house, where eventually my family and Treloar would become very close-knit neighbours. Close neighbours will sometimes have arguments about things. The same would happen, however in a positive manner, when I would have my student reviews at either the school or college. The relationship between my family and Treloar started to click into place and then continued to develop during the first three to four years of my placement when both parties wanted only the absolute best for me. After my very first review, it became much less of a stress for me because I no longer had to worry about continuing to build trust. I just knew after that first review that the trust was naturally happening. It immediately became a great sense of relief and pride, because I wanted to make sure that throughout my time at Treloar I would make the most of what was on offer, as well making the sky my limit.

I am a great believer in the saying "The sky is the limit" because the only person who is responsible for not reaching your dreams is yourself. My advice to you all is: where possible, practise what you preach. Because if I can do it, the kid from the estate, anyone can.

Since the age of ten, I always had a positive and strong-willed nature. Treloar just gave me the platform to be able to unleash my mindset. I would like to think, when you read this memoir, it will allow those of you who are nervous and unsure about whether to believe in your own capacities a helping hand to strengthen **your** mindset. Never let success go to your head and failure get to your heart. Just believe, and it will happen one way or another, just as it did for me when Treloar opened its doors to me for the very first time.

During my time at Treloar, I had many success stories, probably too many to mention. One that particularly sticks out was in Year 10, when the whole year group went to Churchtown in Cornwall for the week, and I abseiled down a cliff for the first time ever in my life. I felt like Bear Grylls with a difference. This was an absolutely astounding achievement for myself and the others in my year group. I have never had such a thrill in all my years of sitting on my bum. However, when an opportunity presented itself, although I was petrified and could not have done it without the rest of my year group, I just had to take it with open arms.

A bit like writing this memoir right here, right now. I feel this is a cracking opportunity to fulfil one of my many dreams, writing a book. Another passion is music. I have always wanted to be a DJ and, more incredibly, a DJ with the use of only one hand. This was an opportunity that presented itself in 2019. The opportunity sprung up to DJ in one of my local bars. You guessed it! I took it without a thought and it ended up being a night, as a music lover, I will never forget. I fulfilled a lifelong dream.

Chapter Five

Challenges

Sport

Potential! What does potential mean? Well, I was about to find out, at four thirty on a Monday afternoon to be precise. At Treloar School, at the end of each school day there was an activity programme as part of the enrichment education they offered. Whilst I was choosing my activities for the term, I came across this funny-looking, funny-sounding word, BOCCIA. Apparently, it was a sport. I thought I had just landed back on earth like ET. So, me being Inspector Morse, I thought 'Let's go and investigate'. Off I went. When I wheeled in, my initial thought was that Hogwarts just gets better and better. What is this I see before me? Lo and behold, it was time to give it a bang. What's the worst that could happen?

Ten minutes into the session, the activity leader, little did I know soon to be a big influence in my life, Sandra King, said, "You have real potential in this sport. Thank you for coming. Would you like to attend one of our school boccia squad training sessions?"

Of course, I said yes! But I didn't jump at the opportunity. After just one experience of that activity with the funny name, I was still adjusting. But the feelings I felt afterwards were strength, determination, nervousness, belief...the list goes on.

Above all else, it was great to have someone that I had never met before now having belief in my sporting abilities.

Some of you may be wondering what I was wondering all those years ago: what the heck is boccia? The best way I can think of to describe boccia is like playing chess but with balls, because the game is all about strategy, hand and eye co-ordination and skill. It is just not as simple as throwing a ball. Boccia is a sport designed for people with physical disabilities but since times change, the governing body of boccia England have now opened it up to a wider spectrum of disabilities, so it is a game for everyone. The game originated in France, and is from the same family as bowls. The sport is predominantly played indoors on a badminton court. Having said that, the game has its own court markings. The balls are made from leather with beads inside them. If you would like to find out more, please visit my web-site *howiroll.com* and click *boccia*.

As the term went on, I got the increasing feeling that the students had the same level of determination and wanted to strive for success as I did. One time, I rolled into the boccia squad training and saw one of the students using assisted technology (commonly known as *the ramp*) to propel the balls, as they did not have use of their upper limbs. Bearing this in mind, their skill and strategy levels were simply astronomical. I couldn't believe what I was seeing from someone whose body was failing them. I thought 'challenge accepted'. From then on, I continued to make my way gradually up the ladder of success in sport. Not bad for someone who got told they couldn't play sport for safety reasons. Tick.

Given my new found beliefs and confidence, the only thing that could be responsible for me not succeeding would be myself. I was determined not to let this happen as much as I could. I began exploring other sporting options that were being offered. As the saying goes, give it a go because you never know. I guess it's my time to put on a show. So here we go!

As the boccia season was drawing ever closer, my nerves were jangling as you can imagine, because it was time for the coaches to make their selection of who would represent the boccia squad at the upcoming tournament in Farnborough. This was a nervous time for me and the rest of the squad. Who would be representing the school? Sure enough, at our next training session, the coach, Sandra King, announced who had been selected. To my utter amazement, I had just been for the very first time in my life selected to represent a team of any kind at any level in sport. OMG! So, I would like to thank Sandra King for getting my sporting journey underway and also making a reality of one of my biggest passions and dreams: to play sport.

After the training session I was on my way back to my boarding house and I still couldn't believe it. I had actually done it. However, I knew I had to keep my feet on the ground and not get too ahead of myself. I also knew that I would be relying on the other athletes with experience to help me through my first ever tournament, competing by myself and representing Treloar School. For someone who wasn't able to compete in sport at any level due to rules and regulations, this was an absolute privilege, honour, and the best thing I had ever done during my short time at Treloar to date.

During the tournament, I could not believe the amount of unity and togetherness within our squad. It was as though I had been with the team for many years. I was able to fit in like I never could have imagined, which for me was a fantastic feeling. Ultimately, I was able to play to my best level at that time, knowing I had the full support from the staff and athletes, whatever my results! Unfortunately, I didn't make the medals. However, it was a valuable experience all the same, one that I learnt a lot from and one I will never forget.

It was now time to get back on the coach for the journey home. I was reflecting on what an amazing day it had been. Even though I didn't achieve the ultimate goal, a medal, what I did achieve far outweighed that; I had gained a new circle of friends.

However, I don't think they would have been well placed if I had needed them on a personal level. I think they would have found that rather challenging, unfamiliar territory. They would not have taken to that side of me, the vulnerable side. Some of you might be wondering what is the difference between a regular friend and a sporting friend. When you are playing sport with your team friends, your non-sporting friends don't necessarily understand the true emotions that lie beneath the competitiveness and the exuberant emotions they see in you – like, the disbelief when you lose – quite as well as that circle of friends you make in a sporting capacity. Team sport friends are able to sympathise with you because, without doubt, we in sport all go through the same emotions.

On the other hand, a regular friend can connect with you personally and you can help each other through everyday struggles. I would say I am at my happiest when I am playing sport, and that is the side of me my sporting friends see. Because my sporting friends only saw me in an upbeat, positive and vibrant mood, I think they would not have quite understood me well as a person when it came to other areas of life. I see sport a bit as my personal counsellor on a daily basis, because it allows me to forget what's going on personally behind closed doors for the duration of whatever sport I may be playing at the time. Sport has also given me a chance to develop my acting skills because, when I am competing, I am a different person. After I've played my sport, it is back to reality and the situation that was bothering me or going on beforehand. These days, I look at what sport has given me in a positive way due to the endorphins and positive vibes that I always get. That is why I said above that I see sport as my personal counsellor. This is still the case to this day.

Although I was only fifteen, myself and Treloar felt there was a lot more to come from my sporting experiences. This became true when, in the summer term, things switched from boccia to athletics. Sandra had a discussion with me about joining the athletics team in the summer term. Once a week during the summer term, regular athletics training sessions started. When I went along, I recognised familiar faces from the boccia team, so immediately felt comfortable in my surroundings. When the sessions began, Sandra asked me to hold what looked like a baseball bat, which was in fact a club. She instructed me how to throw it as far as possible. When I threw the club for the first time, it turned out to be something I was good at. This was noticed by Sandra, so I began my journey towards striving for success in the world of athletics. As the weeks went on, my confidence, not only in my sport but in me as an individual, reached great heights. This confidence enabled me to focus on making stronger those areas I felt were quite weak. It could only have positive outcomes going into my most important years of education. These outcomes served me well, not only as a young fifteen-year-old athlete, but also with regard to my physical condition while going through puberty and with all my hormonal changes. Competing in and playing athletics developed my strength and physical appearance, which in turn made me feel very mentally strong. It made the whole puberty and hormone thing a lot easier to deal with.

In sport there is a term that we use: 'control the controllable'. This means you are only able to control what is going on around you at any given time. For example, you can control how well you play in a match but you cannot control the final outcome or result or the referee's or umpire's decisions. I came to understand that in many ways I can control my own body. If I have the mental strength to deal with my body with all its limitations and changes, internally and externally, this made me feel I had control over the majority of the situation I found myself in. I felt really strong mentally and physically, and, as a consequence, I was able to get through what I think of as my difficult period with minimal fuss.

You are probably wondering how I have made that process seem pretty easy to manage. I would like to assure you that was absolutely not the case. Let's go back to basics and think about how you build a house. Brick by brick. Layer by layer. This is how I have built my mental strength, exactly the same thing just in a different context. I have been through some difficult periods throughout my life. Getting through such periods has been the secret to my developing outstanding mental strength. As the saying goes, what doesn't beat you, makes you stronger. Every bad situation that I have been through I think of as a positive thing – weirdly – because this is adding layers and strengthening my wall so that I will be able to cope mentally in whatever situation is thrown at me. My advice to you all is to try and focus on the good rather than the bad, even if it is the worst situation you have ever found yourself in, because eventually you will be able to look back on that nasty experience and say 'I dealt with that pretty well'. Wouldn't it be good if the next time you are confronted with a nasty situation it will be like water off a duck's back? Stay positive! You can apply this to your sports, remembering you can only control what you do but not what opponents or officials do. Also remember in sport you are not on your own. In most sports it's a team effort, and you can get through more challenging times together as long as you are honest, not only with yourself but also with your team mates and coaches. Don't be too concerned about giving constructive criticism if you feel it is necessary. At the end of the day, everyone is entitled to their opinions, good, bad, or indifferent. Remember this: be firm but fair! Practise and enjoy.

Family challenges

When I started Treloar School, I was what is known as a weekly boarder and would return home at weekends. This continued until Year 9. Once a week, I made a phone call home. On this one specific evening during my weekly call, my mum suggested I become a termly boarder instead of a weekly boarder. When you are a termly boarder you only go home in the holidays, apart from the odd occasional leave weekend.

I have to say this suggestion from my mum didn't particularly sit comfortably with me, as I very much looked forward to returning home for a break each week. Looking on the bright side, when I heard about this new arrangement, I was a boy but by the end of it I was a man. Being a termly boarder taught me to sit on my own two bum cheeks. So effectively I feel very much that from the age of fourteen onwards, I brought myself up. Most fourteen-year-olds are still clinging to their parents and, not surprisingly, are immature. But oh no, not for me. I had to grow up faster than Usain Bolt on a starting block, which, believe it or not, did me a favour.

As the days became months and the months became years,

little did I know what a tough ride I would be in for by the time I was in Year 11. I vividly remember the end of my first term, when I was able to go home. The best way to describe my thoughts and feelings at that time was that I never knew what to expect! During the journey back I noticed my taxi driver took a wrong turn. So I piped up.

"You've gone the wrong way."

"No," he said, "I am taking you to your brother's."

Pure shock! What on earth was going on? For the rest of the journey, I was trying to figure out what was up. I did not expect what I was soon to be told by my brother Darren. If I could have thought a million things, what I was actually told would definitely not have been one of them.

"Hello, mate, you are going to be living with me, at least for the next six months when you come home from school, as your previous address is no longer!"

My brother was telling me this while peeling the vegetables for dinner. My new bedroom was now the living room of my brother's house. During the time I spent with my brother and the household, we built some fantastic bridges and created some wicked memories which I will never forget. They will always hold a special place in my heart, especially the New Year's Eve parties. There's no party better than a Burden party.

However, great parties did not take away the harsh reality of some really hard times ahead. My brother Darren's family home wasn't geared up for my needs and I was getting older, bigger and heavier. It was becoming evident that it was increasingly difficult for my brother to do my personal care, look after my welfare, and keep us both safe in what was then the ongoing set up. Bear in mind that my previous family home – the only one I had ever known – had been set up specifically to cater for my needs, whereas my brother's home simply wasn't.

I will never forget how welcome and part of the family they all made me feel, especially his wife. I can only imagine how hard it was for all of them, knowing the extra equipment that was needed with not enough room to store it. There were already six other people living under the same roof plus me as an addition; all in all, seven people with the added personal care equipment I brought with me. I would just like to say thank you to the whole family for making that episode of my adolescence much, much better and smoother than it could have been.

I am eternally grateful! My brother had taken me under his wing and treated me as his own son at a crucial stage in my life, whether it be going through hormone changes, dealing with GCSEs, or contending with an uncertain future for all of the family. As you can appreciate, it would have been a challenging time for two parents, let alone my brother who had no book guiding him, and was just doing his best in the situation he and we found ourselves in. Me being sixteen, I found this a very difficult and emotional period of my life because I didn't know how to begin to piece together why these circumstances were occurring. The more I thought about it, the more I thought I was dreaming. However, when I opened my eyes, what I saw was the reality. I didn't have much information other than what I had heard the first day of arriving at my brother's house. I could only digest this information one way. I was experiencing every emotion known to man, night or day. But I couldn't share my feelings. It was all going on internally. I tried not to show any emotion outwardly to the public or family or friends. I don't mean I was an expert at not showing emotions because I'm sure people, especially my brother, knew what I was feeling.

When I returned to Treloar to start my college life, one

person that I had known from my Treloar School days, my long-term counsellor from the age of twelve, saw me in the corridor and came up to me.

"Am I right in saying you would like regular counselling sessions? You do not look yourself."

"Yes, please! My head is like an upside down fun fair ride. I would really appreciate support. Thank you very much."

Whilst in my regular therapy, it became apparent that actually what I was going through was psychological trauma. I was told if I didn't get the support that I needed soon, I would be affected on a long-term basis.

A few months after receiving the therapy which it turned out I desperately needed, I settled into a pattern of emotional coping. I was able to suppress my emotions for a week, knowing that the following week I would then have more therapy to let my emotions explode. This enabled me to let my emotions build up to a certain point without it having a damaging effect, because I knew my emotional release would come the following session. As a result, I felt like a new person, able to confront any issues or any worries head on with a clear mind. Crucially, having a clear mind was allowing me to be the person I once was. I started building relationships to quite a deep level with friends, which made me feel internally that I didn't need to rely only on professional help. I could allow my emotions to flow within my circle of friends, which for the majority of the time released positive endorphins and this dramatically improved my state of mind each time I went to my therapy. I found it became easier and easier to cope on a weekly basis.

The big test would be whether I would cope with the situation that landed me in therapy in the first place. The answer is yes. I had much more of a strategy, and coping mechanisms to deal with things that concerned my home life, and which hadn't been sitting comfortably with me. Here is one relevant change that arose from my therapy: I found myself apologising less and less. Before the course of therapy, I would apologise to my brother because, in my mind, I felt like I was in the way or an inconvenience to them.

Another significant change was that I found I was able to voice my opinions to everyone and anyone regardless of whether they liked it or not. Actually, that was another thing my brother taught me but it came out in the therapy as well. Before therapy, I wouldn't voice how I felt, I would just get on with whatever I was asked to do whether I wanted to or not, just for a quiet life. I guess another life lesson is the louder you shout, the easier it is for you to be heard and the more stuff you will be able to achieve. So never be worried or ashamed to ask for professional support if you need it. There is always light at the end of the tunnel.

When my brother and I were looking for an alternative residence, because of these changes in myself, I was able to look at things from a much clearer perspective. All I needed was to clear the emotional garbage that was in my way in order to be able to achieve successes, even throughout that difficult time at college. I was mightily relieved to be back to creating my success story at college which continued day by day, month by month, year by year, until the end. I had started with two problems, but one of these was now solved, my emotional confusion. That left me to deal with the one remaining big issue: finding suitable accommodation, as my family home no longer was suitable, given I was nearly seventeen years old. Weirdly, I had no worries about what I was going to face, as I had my big brother as my rock and his family on my side and I had a clear mind. I was ready for anything...

… Until we went to view the social worker's proposed permanent arrangement for my residence, which was, safe to say, no way appropriate! When Darren and I went for the viewing, we walked in to greet the manager. No word of a lie, I thought I was entering Marwell Zoo! I was hearing noises that you would only expect to hear at a zoo. And the youngest resident was fifty years old while I was a mere seventeen! So, having viewed the placement and not taken too long to decide it wasn't appropriate, back to the drawing board we went.

Thank goodness we found an outstanding placement. Mind you, it took us somewhere between three and six months, if memory serves me right! This placement was a very intimate care setting with only three other residents. It was almost like walking into someone else's home, rather than your typical care home. This didn't stop me from having my initial doubts. However, as soon as I got speaking to the manager and staff members, I felt relaxed and comfortable in what potentially could be my new place of residence. Darren and I spent around an hour having a look round, asking any questions we wanted, after which we left and returned home. Over dinner, we had a discussion on what we had seen, and we came to the same conclusion that Future Care was to be my new long-term placement for the next two years.

Again, I would just like to thank my brother and his wife and family and the part they played in solving my two problems (my mind and my placement), and also my counsellor at Treloar who indeed played a very important part in my emotional recovery. If it wasn't for you, magical people, I couldn't have got through this more-than-challenging period of my life. So, thank you very much. I will never forget it.

Since this sensitive episode in my life, I think of my brother more as a father figure than as a brother.

I will always be grateful for the support you have shown me, especially carrying out the roles of two parents at once. I don't think I will ever meet a man quite like you ever again in my life. You're one in a million. Not only did you teach me right from wrong, you also gave me a valuable lesson in how to look after myself financially. Even though at the time I thought you were being rather annoying, as it was MY money! That being said, looking back on it now, again I thank you very much for being gratefully annoying. Thanks to you, I would no longer go into Alton and buy myself a lunch and dinner at Subway or Dominoes, as I knew all my bank statements would come to you, and, as you remember, very soon you kindly threatened if I carried on the way I was going financially destroying my future you would take the dreadfully scary step of activating Power of Attorney. This would mean I would have to ask my brother even if I wanted to spend just a pound!

Training with England

Anyway, enough about my hormone changes, let's get on to talking about the real stuff, which is my progress within athletics. As the summer term was proceeding, I am pleased to tell you so were my athletics. We were now quite far into training, leading towards competitions of the season. For those of you who aren't aware, I am a full-time wheelchair user so running, jumping, skipping, and sprinting are all out of the question. So, you may be wondering whether athletics can offer me very little! I have no qualms and I am proud to say if you were thinking this, you are 101% wrong, as indeed everything can be adapted even if you do it all sitting on your bum. The disciplines I took up in athletics were in the field section; that is, for those of you who aren't very

49

on top of your sport, all the disciplines that are in the throwing category and are carried out on the field. All those other aspects like running, sprinting and hurdling are carried out on the track. In essence, athletics is split into two divisions: track and field. I was lucky enough to be able to compete in the field division, throwing my club and something called height bean bag. Height bean bag is not measured by distance but measured on the clearance of a high jump bar. At each height you get three attempts. I used to compete regionally and nationally in this event for which I have won numerous medals. I thoroughly enjoyed it. My first competitive event, which was extra special for me, and one I will always have fond memories of, was in Woking, again representing Treloar and myself.

This moment was extra special as not only was I competing competitively in boccia, I was now doing it in athletics, which I very much enjoyed, especially when I became one of the more senior members of both teams, as my older peers started to move on to the college. I was now able to become a role model for those younger athletes who were just starting their journey. I had been there myself just a few years earlier. It felt strange but amazing all at the same time because I was someone they looked up to. It was a humbling experience, as I was used to being the one looking up at people, being the youngest in my family. It was weird having the roles reversed. Nevertheless, my new role was one I took very seriously, and I dedicated myself to being the best role model I could be for the younger ones, especially when it came to competitions. I felt that my role didn't just apply within sport. I wanted to be a role model for them during my education, especially my GCSE years. Hopefully, I did a good job at being a role mode. I can certainly tell you I tried my absolute best even in the tough times when it would have been quite easy to blow my fuse. However, as a role model, nine times out of ten I managed to diffuse my frustrations and stop fuse-blowing from occurring. This being a role model became a distraction from my troubles.

However, the distraction didn't stop me from thinking negative things, nor my concern that I wouldn't be able to cope with juggling the two things, being a role model and my GCSEs. My role did not stop me from occasionally thinking about blowing my fuse. I knew that if I blew my fuse, not only would it have an impact on myself, it would also have an impact on the younger people. They would think that is the right way to react to times when things are not going your way. For example, if I had a bad exam result and I reacted badly, they would think that was the appropriate way to react if that happened to them. It was about getting the right balance between suppressing your emotions and remembering, before you blow your fuse, that you are a role model to those people looking up to you.

I guess there is a time and a place to deal with your negative moods and that time and place was Treloar's very own **secret garden**. This garden is not a fantasy. The secret garden had been designed by Treloar's grounds staff for a place where students could have time for reflection and let out their emotions whilst surrounded by local nature, fishponds, and water fountains. Every evening, I used to take some time, an hour or so, in the secret garden just to reflect on the day I'd had. It was here I'd let out some negative emotions, as I knew it was a safe place to do so.

This garden was very influential on me managing to carry out my two responsibilities, role model and GCSE student.

For me, sport was a bit of a comfort blanket after my day of studying for my exams. I could use sport as my down time, if I fancied a change from my place of reflection, the secret garden. Especially being fifteen and sixteen, it was rather a lot to cope with: exams, being away from home for the first time, and not forgetting being adolescent and all the challenges that come along with that. Being a role model, having a place for reflection and also playing sport in down time was a successful combination for me to get through these tough periods in life.

I am not saying my plan of action will work for everyone, but action-planning is something I feel very passionate about. It is vitally important that you set yourself step by step goals that are easy to achieve, and if you need to let out some emotion, you cater for that in your plan as well. **My** plan covered the sports I chose and the secret garden. By having things set in place, organised by yourself, the plan may help as a distraction when you are going through tough times or need something to focus your mind. Having your own plan is, in my opinion, a successful way to roll through life. When I say having a plan for yourself, this doesn't mean taking my plan, as it may not work for you – but by all means, you can give it a try and see how you go. Putting in a sufficient personal plan means you as an individual coming up with a plan, something that you organise and you feel comfortable with, and most of all, find fun. At least then when you carry out your plan, whatever it may be, you can be assured it will make you feel good at the end. A smile a day, that's what I say!

Why I had my plan, as I have mentioned before, was because I was now playing two sports at a reasonably high level, and as it was at a reasonably high level, a bit of enjoyment dwindled away, as it was always likely to do because of the nature and level I was competing at. My plan enabled me to see the fun side of sport whilst maintaining my competitive edge, both very important if

I were to keep the mind and body ticking over. The enjoyment that I felt was being replaced by the feeling of fighting for a place, or indeed keeping my place in whatever training or competition I was in. An example I can give you comes from one weekend I went to a Treloar training day for boccia. I was tasked with trying to knock into balls rather than just rolling up, in other words deflecting off a ball to achieve my goal. I found this a very challenging exercise, mentally and physically. My enjoyment was being replaced by hard work. The higher the competition, the more pressure I felt. Having said that, I always went back to my roots and tried to remember why I started the sport in the first place. And that was to enjoy it!

Sure enough, after taking some advice from players and coaches alike, not forgetting advice from myself, I started to enjoy it again and at the same time get some impressive results, which in turn developed into an honourable selection to train with the England team! Before my selection to train with the team, I had to perform well and train well on a consistent basis, both in regional and national events. If you wanted to be successful, this was the path to go down: dedication, belief, enjoyment and consistency in performance and results. This is what led to my selection.

Tension was building, alongside the excitement, at the thought of training with my country's squad of players. However, I knew if I wanted to be successful, I had to keep my wheels firmly on the ground and not start pulling wheelies before I knew what had hit me. The day before setting off for the national training weekend arrived, so off I went on my four-hour journey up to the camp. This was a proud moment, not only for me but also for my brother as this was his first ever experience of seeing me play boccia. What a place for him to start!

I will never forget the journey on the way up, because it was a boiling hot day and we were stuck in traffic for about two to three hours. Put it this way, it was enough time for my brother to get out of the van and have a cigarette sitting on the tarmac of one of the busiest motorways in the world. Not everyone can say they have done that. Pretty extraordinary, wouldn't you say? After the blockage on the motorway, it was time to resume our mammoth journey. We eventually arrived safe and sound at our hotel, very tired, yet optimistic and positive for the day ahead.

After a good night's sleep, it was breakfast time. I had never consumed so much breakfast before a big day, but I knew a full English would enhance my chances of a good session. I would like to add I did have a healthy bowl of fruit, alongside my hearty full English. Whilst eating, some of the England team started to appear in the breakfast hall. This moment was really strange, as I felt my role modelling days were quite a way behind me and I was back to square one. They were **my** role models and people for me to look up to. The energy that was pulsing through my veins was incredible. It was as though someone had given me a life supply of sherbet lemons. Buzzing wasn't the word! Still buzzing, I now had to get loaded for training, so it was into the van we went. After around ten or twenty minutes, we started to approach the training venue. I have to tell you, even though I was still in the van, this was the proudest moment I have ever had, still to this day. On arrival, I had never seen so many disability vehicles in one place. Eventually, we found parking after driving round in circles. We parked up, unloaded the equipment I needed for training, and unloaded myself. On approaching the venue, it was as if I had never seen these coaches or played boccia in my life. I had never seen such a professional side to the sport. Even though I knew some of the England players and coaching staff, the atmosphere at this training weekend was like no other – in a good way, though.

When I pushed my joystick over the line into the training hall, my buzziness changed to nervousness. I knew, with my positive attitude and outlook in life in general, I would be fine. It's how you channel those nerves, and do not let the nerves channel you. Off I went to warm up, sticking to my normal routine. I thought my routine was complicated and a lot for my assistant (Darren, my brother) to help me with but, my God, I was wrong! My warm up was relatively simple compared with the rather scientific and in-your-face warm-ups I was privileged to see around me. Let's just say, food for thought. During the warm-up I felt like a complete novice and, I asked myself, how the hell were these athletes throwing the shots that were being thrown? I have been in some good competitions and matches but this was on another level. I knew with hard work, dedication, self-belief and guidance, there would be no reason, other than my body tightening up, why I could not be at the same level. Let's face it, I must be pretty near or they would not have selected me. If you would like to know more about warm-ups, make sure you keep reading to the end.

After the warm-up, it was time for a debrief, so we all huddled together and were told how the day was going to unfold. Pretty standard, you would think…Until all the athletes were put into small groups in our classifications according to the extent of our disabilities, ready to compete with each other. It consisted of different challenges and scenarios in the game which, believe it or not, was a fun experience. Some of you might think that weird, calling training 'fun', but it is when you are all at the same level, consistently throwing world-class shots. The fun part was seeing and laughing at the coaches trying to work out who was closest.

I have never seen so many coaches trying to make a simple decision. Who was closest? Red or blue? It can't be that hard surely!

After skills training, it was time for those athletes to get together with the coaches who went on to explain why we were there, which I found really inspiring to hear. It made me want more. The coaches told us that they believed that we were the best players in the country, so deserved our chance.

"It's up to you as athletes whether you take the chance given to you through our selection process."

With those words ringing in my ears, I felt optimistic but at the same time pressured more than I had previously experienced. For the first time in a long while, I started to doubt myself. The way I would describe pressure is: it is your best friend and your worst enemy rolled into one. I began the daunting task of fighting two things: positive pressure and negative pressure. I kept telling myself negative pressure is just a feeling, not reality. I stuck to this mantra throughout the weekend whilst learning a lot from what some of the best and most talented athletes and coaches had to offer in the sport of boccia.

I would like to say a little bit about what it is like having a boccia training session over a whole weekend. For sure, I was used to weekly training sessions. I did, however, slightly underestimate what was involved in training for a full weekend. Nonetheless, I took a lot of positivity out of it, and I knew I needed to do more work on my stamina to be able to endure such a physically demanding weekend in the future, if I was lucky enough to be asked to return. One thing I can definitely take away from the experience as a whole is that it was definitely an eye-opener about high level sport. If you are an athlete, but also like eating chocolate and cream cake, I advise you strongly to cut this out, as much as possible, as this hinders your performance and health, which was certainly the case for me. For medical reasons, I had been put on a full fat diet by a Treloar dietician, so I had to find substitutes for the chocolate and cream cakes. These substitutes came in the form of Ensure and Fortisip build-up drinks. Let me tell you, they didn't have the same effect on my taste buds as chocolate and cream cakes but they do say: if it doesn't taste nice, it's doing you good! If you want to reach high levels in sports, you will need to make lifestyle changes such as stopping lying in bed and going to the gym, eating healthily – and that doesn't include popcorn! However, it does include being committed to giving your body the greatest chance of achieving your best performance.

For those athletes among you who get selected to represent your country, and who have an assistant supporting them who knows next-to-nothing about the sport, it is your job to make sure that assistant receives clear, to-the-point advice and is provided with a good understanding of the rules and regulations in order to stop any violations occurring in competitions and training. Look at things from the perspective of your assistant, and pay him or her the same respect you would pay another athlete, because it is just as hard for the assistant as it is you, when that person has never assisted on a boccia court and, even more so when it is at national competitions.

Chapter Six

Moving On

Friends

In my opinion, **friends** is the best word in the dictionary, because you can roll out every emotion we as humans feel day-in, day-out, but your friendship will see you through it all. Laughter, sadness, celebrations and failures, all of this and more, and, above all, without judging you. The best thing about friends is that you can choose them. I would like to think that I have quite a good reputation for making friends. As a friend to many people, I believe it is important to say how you feel, at any time and in any situation. This is what true friendship is all about! I would like to give a special mention to a few of my friends and brothers.

When I was at Treloar School, you may remember me previously mentioning in my book walking into a hall with some lads playing hockey. One of those lads was Shane. From the moment we met in that hockey hall, I knew we could have a friendship that would last a lifetime and beyond. I can remember lots and lots and lots of funny memories, none more so than when we both got grounded to the boarding house for breaking time curfews. We both thought it would be hilarious to get assisted into our pyjamas, and act as if we were sticking to our punishment until it was all quiet. Then we decided to go and play hockey in our pyjamas, like two naughty little schoolboys in the playground. It was fair to say at that time in our young lives we thought we were indestructible, so decided to ignore the house's advice and just come back before our manager found out! Luckily, there was a pane of glass opposite the hockey hall so students could see round the corner who was coming up the pathway. Unfortunately, or fortunately, I spun round to take a shot for Shane to save and missed the ball. I spun round so fast I ended up opposite the pane of glass. Out of the corner of my eye I could see a man, who very much looked like our care manager, coming towards the boarding house.

So, I turned to Shane and said, "Oi, Badger (Shane's nickname), drop your stick, you need a head start because the manager is coming and your chair is so slow! You need a head start!"

Shane's escape was thanks to me and my bumper car. I gave Shane a nudge from behind to make him quicker. I am glad to say we never got caught by the manager because of my little nudge. All's well that ends well, as they say! I can honestly say there was something rather special about our friendship/bromance because, even when we argued, more often than not, nine times out of ten, we laughed with and at each other, even in the most testing times when we were meant to be serious!

Shane and I always took banter to a higher level, sometimes too far for people to cope with. When we went to a KFC near the college in Basingstoke, we decided to have a food fight with the leftover food that people didn't want. We were bored. It was a food fight. If you were a bystander watching two disabled guys having a food fight throwing KFC at each other, or trying to, it is possibly one of the funniest things you could ever watch. Or so it seemed to us. I would just like to apologise to a lady whose baby I hit with some popcorn chicken.

Sorry!

Lads will be lads! Brothers will be brothers! It is fair to say you could not leave me and Shane in the same room alone for five minutes before we were up to no good. But, hey, always look on the bright side. At least we weren't letting our disabilities get in the way of being young lads or overshadowing our personalities and our ability to make the most serious situations into the funniest of jokes. This friendship with Shane I am never going to forget, one I will always cherish with nothing but good memories, happiness and laughter.

Until we meet again. RIP brother!

Freeing from the nest

For many years, I had been cocooned in the safety of various care homes and settings. As you know, my first ever experience of living away from home was Treloar School. That feeling I had when I first started my week away from home all those years ago, still to this day, is the one that sticks out the most. It is my favourite memory because it made me the independent and successful man I am today.

I had often wondered whether I would get the same feeling when it was time to make the next transition, from Treloar School to Treloar College, but I guessed only time would tell. I kept thinking I had plenty of time on my hands but, in reality, days and hours go so fast and, before you know it, time's up. I always tried my best to have me-time so I could at least try to get my head around the possible outcomes. However, I tried not to think too deeply, because I knew I had to choose my GCSE subjects before I could think about anything else. All of my thinking went on choosing wisely, subjects I would actually enjoy, rather than spending the rest of my school days a 'misogs'. What I found really useful was that Treloar did things slightly differently from the average school. During the process of choosing our exam subjects, they carefully created the groups we would study in, whatever class or form we were in. It didn't always work out. One particular student was one of the last students in the group to choose one of the most popular subjects so, amusingly, there wasn't enough room for him to take that subject. He had to choose history whilst everyone else was having fun, occasionally outdoors, studying PE. All I can say on that one is 'Unlucky!'

After choosing my subjects, it was time to do the preparation work. I would just like to point out I never knew how much reading was involved and my neck would ache as a result of reading so many text books. It's a pity that iPhones weren't quite up to the standard they are now, otherwise I could have had half of the textbooks read to me by an American voice. Luckily, these days I don't tend to get that problem and there is not a text book in sight. But if I was to use it, my iPhone would be my best friend: #lazy. I would say the preparation stage was quite enjoyable due to the fact we had, as Year 10s, certain responsibilities, if you can call them that. As we were in GCSE year, we were allowed to have our classrooms open for our use until 10.30 pm. Now I have left and it has been many, many years since those days, I would like to inform those teachers and senior management that, when you get a bunch of students together who really get on well, not a lot of studying goes on. I really learnt how to play online games. If they had a GCSE in gaming, I would have no problem getting an A*. I can safely say, though, the reason I got good GCSE results generally, in my opinion, was due to the fact that we were all able to study together, regardless of whether we were in the same form or not. When we did get down to study and got stuck, we could support each other with whatever was needed.

Sometimes we would use one another's skills to complete tasks that needed completing. So, for instance, there were a couple of students in our study group with good enough hand function and dexterity to be able to write with chunky pens. And if our computers crashed, due to too much gaming, we had the students who could write to fall back on, which is always a good plan. I would admit that if I had been studying on my own maybe I could have been the next Stephen Hawking. However, I am glad I wasn't studying on my own, as I was able to, like I said previously, enjoy studying as part of a group. Part of the Treloar regime was to put those students with all different kinds of skill sets together. For instance, you would get students who were good at IT in with students who were not quite as confident, so if there was an IT problem those students capable could fix the problem nine times out of ten. However, let's not forget we were teenagers so that did not stop us from being mischievous and leaving the groups we were put in and joining groups our friends were in. I am glad to say, certainly in **my** Year 10/11 experience, the teachers never found out, until now when they read this section of my memoir. I'm sorry!

After months of studying and being in our groups, it was time to get serious and start answering questions in exams on what we had been revising … scary! One of the good things about having a disability is that you get extra time when doing exams, so if you are having a dumb moment, you can use your extra time to good effect (hopefully) and, when finally putting down your answer on paper, it might just show you're brainier than you were an hour ago. During my exams, I would have someone called a scribe. However, on this particular day I was not expecting to have one particular teacher helping me with my science exam.

This is what happens when there are not enough hands to go round. On this occasion, luckily for me, I was taking my science exam and had my science teacher as my scribe. I thought 'This time I have landed on my wheels! Here's my chance to land my first A*!'

However, I was soon to be disappointed because I only got one almighty nudge during the whole hour exam. Cheers, mate! I would have paid you later!

Now on to my favourite subject: PE. Physical Education. My Year 11 PE experience was one I would never ever forget, due to the fact the teacher got us to predict our results. We all (apart from one student) predicted we would get Ds. To the class's amazement, when the results came back, we actually surprised ourselves. We all got Cs. I guess that must mean we were good students after all. It was really nice to exceed the teacher's expectations. I have never enjoyed a subject so much in my life. Enjoyment brings with it success! As a consequence, many years later, I am now a qualified disability sports coach. So, kids, choose wisely. I believe that there is a time and a place to be mischievous. You just have to pick your moments. If I am honest with you, when I was studying for my Physical Education exam, I did not mess around once. I believe this is what led to exceeding the teacher's predictions, something I am still proud of to this day.

Moment of truth

There was a huge sense of anticipation before the big moment of truth. Some students, including myself, were anxiously waiting to see if our funding had been approved to go up to Treloar College. As well as waiting nervously, I was also freaking out because I knew I was going to be leaving such a comfort blanket.

I had been used to how the house staff and the various departments managed my care needs. The house staff, in particular, were important to me, as naturally you build a bond and a rapport with those individuals. It is surprisingly hard knowing you are going to have to let them go in a few months. It is an overwhelming feeling, especially when they have assisted you through some of the most traumatic moments of your childhood. I built such strong relationships with some staff that I could even tell who each one was just from the way they knocked on my door in the mornings or evenings. The psychological bonds would never fade away – they were just too strong.

Even though most students who knew me and saw me on a daily basis didn't really know about my sensitive side, thinking about leaving them actually caused me to become anxious and a little uptight. I didn't know how I would react leaving those people I had built such strong bonds with. What made it easier and less of a war zone in my head was the fact that I would still have the same counsellor that I had when I started, all those years ago, as my therapist worked at both sites. I managed to get through this rather alien period by having regular sessions with my counsellor on transferring from the school to the college. When it was the actual time to leave, I had an almighty flashback to when I was leaving my home and family for the first time. It felt near enough identical. However, the way I dealt with having to leave such a place, inwardly told me how much I had matured over the years of their expert support. Thank you!

Summer holiday and the last weeks with my brother and his family

All my new family unit could do was stick together, no matter how hard things would get. I knew we would get through

64

somehow. As the weeks went on, I knew I was getting closer to starting college. Now, knowing my funding was all secure, in a way, I was counting down the days to my start date. This wasn't because the time at my brother's was bad. This was because I knew he was finding it increasingly difficult to cope with my disability, due to the fact his house wasn't geared up for it. So, when the day finally arrived for me to start my new adventure, I found this an incredible relief, as I knew my brother, and more so his family, would get a much-needed break from lifting me up and down the stairs every day. Nearly nine weeks of that, and more, takes its toll on anyone. I always knew my brother wanted the best for me so he never complained, but I can pretty much guarantee there were plenty of times he must have wanted to scream, especially as the situation we were in became clearer. But the point is he never batted an eyelid. He just got on with it, like the true warrior that I know he is.

I would like to be honest with you. I found this situation a very, very tough battle, almost the same as a drug addict fighting an addiction. I was just fighting with my feelings and emotions because, even though I had eight, nearly nine weeks, to digest things with my brother and the family, I hadn't even reached the tip of the iceberg, so when I started college my behaviour became somewhat unusual and erratic, almost like I had developed ADHD overnight. It wasn't till six months into my first year at college I began to receive very intensive therapy and get to the bottom of my behaviour and how erratic I was being. My therapy consisted of dealing with feelings, thoughts, and scenarios. After several months of intensive support to do with my emotions and anger, it was revealed that I had a very mild form of post-traumatic stress disorder. This was what was causing my meltdowns.

Leaving Shane behind

I saw Shane as a brother. This might seem a weird concept to many people, but the truth of the matter is you really had to understand the way we both just connected so naturally. It was like we were born into the same family, living separately during the holiday periods, but nonetheless distance didn't stop us being there for one another in the ups and downs of everyday life. We both had extraordinary amounts of trust in each other, so we would tell things to each other that you would only expect our biological families to need to know. Our relationship was so good that sometimes we told our deep problems only to each other and not even our families! I am pleased to say this extraordinary and incredible brotherly bond continued throughout my transition between leaving Treloar School and starting Treloar College just down the road. Even though Shane was still playing catch up and going into Year 11 at the school, we still managed, if not every day then most days, to contact each other either by phone, email, or social media, more often than not, if we could get away with it. Not begrudgingly, and sorry, teachers, we did it.

This continued throughout my first year at college and his last year at Treloar School until he also made the move from the school to the college. At last, we were back together. I expect the college students and staff didn't know what was going to hit them when Shane and me started our antics at the more senior level. Our antics stepped up a level or three, especially when we were both able to go out independently without staff intervention when we both passed our road skill assessments. But now, I want to mention a new person who entered my life early into the first year at college.

Chapter Seven

Frankie

My first year of college was not much different from when I left off at school, other than the surroundings. I guess having already been at the school for a number of years stood me in good stead for college life and made the transition that little bit smoother. The thing that also impacted on the smoothness is that some of my friends from my school were coming up with me, which, looking back on it, was quite a special bonus! For those of you who feel uncomfortable making a transition from school to college, my advice to you is if you have experienced a transfer which worked, is stick to the same routine. For me, that meant unpacking my stuff, putting it away, and listening to my music to let people know I had arrived in style. When I arrived for my first year at college, little did I know that I was actually going to be sharing with an old school friend, which felt rather nostalgic, given we had already quite a lot in common. Instead of feeling like a first-year student, in actual fact very early on I felt like a third-year student due to the way I was able to settle in!

I was very comfortable with my new surroundings, so it was time for me to go exploring round the college to see if I felt any different or more grown up. I spent a good hour bombing around, having a butcher's at every little thing, almost forgetting about dinner. My attitude at this point was not to worry about college mealtimes – I am a big boy now; I can ring Dominoes! Truth be told, this was what I did, and so at the end of my first day I was yet to experience the true taste of college food. I don't class the food I was given when I had visited the college before the end of my schooldays as genuine college food, as from my experience they make an effort when they know they have a new student day on the horizon!

My first taste of college grub the next day was something of an experience. It was breakfast time when I met for the very first time a young lady called Francesca and breakfast would never be the same again. Her first words to me were:

"You look normal. You are not making noises like a farm animal, so could I sit at your table?"

"OK," I said. "Nice to meet you too. Why not!"

I began to explore the reasons for the out-there attitude behind what she had just said. It was something I could easily relate to, as I had thought something very similar when I first started Treloar School. Reader, you will remember that I had not been around a vast amount of people with various conditions and disabilities, so I could get her point of view straightaway! Because I was able to understand and relate to Frankie's thought process and feelings, our friendship began to develop at the speed of light! Over my rather rubbery bacon roll, we began to get to know each other and quickly realised we were kind of cut from the same cloth.

It was a turning point for me. I started to think about myself in terms of what my own capabilities could be and have subsequently turned out to be. However, to realise this, it sometimes helps to have people around you from similar circumstances and backgrounds to yourself in order for that deeper side to come out. I realised all this when I heard Frankie's very first remarks to me. I knew that I could relate to Frankie in

68

the way that she was feeling, and I wanted to do my best not to palm her off, but rather to show my support and that I had been in her shoes on a previous occasion! I was thinking to myself that this is a very déjà vu situation, and I was 99.9% sure I could get to the bottom of it. We spent the next hour or so reliving our similar experiences through conversation, which I have to say was very strange because it was like we were the male and female of each other. In life, there is no truer saying that you never stop learning. I definitely learned something very extraordinary and the way I explained this, to myself, was to say that I had found actually a female version of me. Yes, I know what you are thinking. How can there be two Adams, albeit a female version? But the fact was that, after a very interesting and rubbery breakfast, I was quite shell-shocked to learn how similar we were, not only because of our circumstances but also as people. This was fascinating to say the least, and I couldn't wait to share the next three years of college life with the female version of myself... Exciting times ahead!

That evening, we continued to share and swap stories with each other, as I was still absolutely flabbergasted at how freakishly similar we were, especially how we both connected and could sometimes fathom out exactly what each other were thinking just by facial expressions, without verbally communicating anything! As the evening went on, I was really excited to test out if I was able to communicate with Frankie without others around us knowing what was going on but I guess it was too early to say. I'm sure that moment would come somewhen in our three years at college together. Over time, if we were stressed or upset about something and we wanted to tell each other exactly how we felt but didn't want to broadcast it, we would use code words that only myself and Frankie knew. For example, if something was bad our codeword was 'bogies'. If something was good our codeword was 'fabulous'. I can imagine what some of you must be thinking. Don't worry. Yes, we did get some really funny looks, especially if we were around people that knew us well, if the looks are as I remember. I can imagine how fast your brains are wracking as to how this communication is even a possibility!

We often got up to all sorts of mischief, especially when we were on various holiday placements together. Due to circumstances, occasionally the social services would have to pay for me to go to a place called Vitalise. This is a place that gives people with disabilities the chance to experience a holiday week within the UK for a short break, paid for by the local authority if that's where the funding comes from. It turned out Frankie's and my situations would become even more bizarrely similar because our personal circumstances, the fact we could not return to our family homes, meant the local authorities and social workers had to pay for a Vitalise holiday placement when the college was closed for half term. Our first holiday placement meant we travelled from Treloar to Manchester together on the train. Later there would be other destinations, such as Nottingham. Using our traffic light safety tests put in place by the college, together we managed to get up north, where they speak funny, in one piece. So, let the fun begin!

Personally, I knew this travel around the country was in reality going to be a really tough test and would help me work out whether independence was really for me or not. I guess you could say it's the closest I would ever come to *SAS: Who Dares Wins*. Luckily, I have always had my independent mind to support me in the toughest of situations. Not only did I have my independent mind, I also had the female version of myself by my side. Two Adams is more than enough brain power to take on the mighty Manchester. However, on the journey to Manchester myself and Frankie actually somewhat bumped against each other. In other words, our ways of handling it didn't always line up. All I kept thinking was, I must get there in one piece. My way of doing a major journey from the south to the north is to be focussed, vigilant, and switched on, simply because you never know what's going to happen, especially on a journey you've never been on before. I knew my concentration levels would have to be at their highest they had been in a very, very long time. Normally, if it was a familiar journey, I would chat till the cows came home, as I know point-for-point what to do and where to go, so apologies to Frankie if my responses to some of your jokes and questions were very vague. I wasn't ignoring you. I was simply trying to stay alive.

For young lads and lasses, or even older folk, never be worried at how people may be perceiving you when you are trying to do a not-to-be-messed-around task and stay alive, even if when you are travelling you are normally the life and soul of the journey. Remember this: on journeys you are comfortable with, that's when you can be the life and soul. On the other hand, when it's a journey with lots of pressure, you have to think **safety first** and turn into a creature people won't be expecting. When friends are laughing and joking and you are trying to be as serious as the Statue of Liberty, if they are any kind of friends, they will surely understand why you're being the way you are. Simply say, "I'm saving my life." Don't worry. They will understand. A week is plenty of time to have a crack (a laugh). If you are normally the relaxed kind, when travelling, you could always make up for the banter and laughter on the way back, because you've done it once before, or several times, and you now know the route and

71

where you are going. It's just when travelling, it only takes a split second for your eye to go off the ball and you are bang, in trouble. Just keep focussed, and you will get where you need to get safe and sound. Safe and sound is better than being in a compound!

Once Frankie and I had arrived and I stopped being as serious as Simon Cowell on *Britain's Got Talent* minus the high trousers, I began to relax and give Manchester some of the southern vibes they had been missing. But because they were so hardened in their Mancunian ways, it was very tough to get them to crack a little smile. However, by the time the week came to an end, they couldn't stop laughing and we both got called 'southern fairies' to which I responded:

"There must be plenty of PG Tips round here as you all look like the chimp on the advert, you Northern monkeys!"

Having stayed in Manchester, I can well recommend the city, as it's one of the most wheelchair friendly destinations to be in, in my opinion. The people, although sometimes there's a lingo barrier, are some of the most helpful and genuine you would ever meet, so I felt rather comfortable and would go back at any time. Great place. It's even better for those of you who are Manchester United fans and enthusiasts. I recommend taking the tour of the Old Trafford Stadium, as you will learn all about the history up to the present day, so it is well worth a view. This was on a day when our people providing our accommodation took the residents on a shopping trip to the Trafford centre. Me and Frankie, being the independent darlings that we are, decided to be spontaneous and do our own thing, as long as we didn't miss the coach back. That's when we discovered the Old Trafford stadium tour and decided to go on it. Being a Chelsea fan, this was quite a hard moment, stepping into one of our most bitter rival's houses. All I could think of doing was showing off the

Chelsea shirt I was wearing at the time.

"You guys need to support a real team."

However, the reason you are seeing me alive today is because I decided against this. All jokes aside, the access in and around the stadium is unbelievable. So please, if the opportunity ever arises, don't let it evaporate. Take it. I am pleased to say we made it back to our bus, with much laughing and joking, with three minutes to spare. On the journey back to our accommodation, I was hungry and had cookies on my lap. No one told us no food was to be consumed on the journey. So, I was munching away on a cookie, only for one of the staff to come up

"You are not supposed to be eating on any journey by minibus."

"Oh, I wasn't aware of this and anyway it's got my medication in it. It's called a high fat diet."

You can imagine the response I got! It would have been worse if I hadn't offered him a piece of my cookie, mind you. As a result, I was able to keep munching and stick to my 'diet', so happy days!

I would like to think throughout the time I was in Manchester, I had a positive impact on those people who aren't so confident and comfortable with their conditions and was able to show them that just because you have a condition or a disability, **life still goes on**. If I even got that message through to one person, that's job done for me!

Chapter Eight

Overcoming

Road skill assessment

For those of you who are not familiar with this, road skill assessment is a process that every college student goes through to determine their safety and abilities to drive their wheelchairs/scooters independently in the local community or further afield. It all depends on your level of skills. If assessments go well, the students are able to go out, providing they follow a route they've been assessed for by an occupational therapist (OT). To work out levels of students' capability, OTs used something known to students as a **traffic light system**. If students are on **red,** this means they are dependent on staff support if they want to go off campus. If students are on **amber,** this means students are able to go off campus independently, however must only go on the routes they have been assessed for. Finally, if students are on **green,** this means these students go on something called the transport programme. This is an assessment carried out to a more advanced level, which includes travelling to London on a train. If students were lucky enough to pass the assessment, the students would then be able to go anywhere they choose without staff intervention. However, if those students are spotted doing unsafe practice, this could result in their privilege being taken away and having to start again!

I went through these assessments, and I am thrilled to say that I was one of those students who managed to get the green light, much to the amazement of the OTs, house staff, and I am pretty sure, although he might not know until now, my brother. For those young lads and lasses still dependent on adults to go out, I know from first-hand experience that freedom and independence are everything, especially when you are reaching the age when you are legally allowed to consume alcohol on a regular basis. When I say 'regular basis', I want to assure you I did this only at the weekends, not every day. As far as independent travel is concerned, nothing is given on a plate or for free. It is particularly true for your assessment at the highest level of independence, i.e. the transport programme – green on the traffic light system. This programme can be a daunting and full of pressure. Not a stone is unturned because, let's face it, the moment they let us loose our lives are at risk. OTs have to be 100,000% sure that you will be as safe as a Roman stone building. Every mistake you make is picked over with a fine-toothed comb, for example crossing a road at a blind corner is heavily analysed and scrutinised, as I found out on my very first experience of the programme. I thought I would just do what I always did or used to do when at home. This proved to be the wrong attitude to take, as it turned out that none of what I had been doing was safe enough to allow me to go out on my own. More safe practice in their eyes was needed. It must have worked because I am still alive. But not the pedestrians (only kidding!)

I thoroughly enjoyed the experienced of the testing programme, but it is for sure not to be underestimated. It was one of the most challenging aspects of college life for me, but at the end of the day I am glad and relieved to have got through it and passed at green level – not like several students who had the ability to go green but underestimated it, so stayed on red-man-dead-man. I suppose I went into this situation naïve, as I was already doing independent tasks when on those rare occasions I got to go home, and went shopping or went out in the community in general.

My idea of road safety I now know was completely wrong, compared to the standard of an OT at Treloar. Like we all do, I thought it would be as easy as pie and a breeze, knowing that I already had experience of going out by myself. This was completely the wrong attitude to have. Just because you have experience... well it might be the wrong kind of experience, not one experts or specialists are looking for. So please go into your tests with an open mind, ready to be scrutinised and be put on the spot on every point of risk. But all the same, have fun, enjoy it and practise.

Life is a risk

From the time I entered the world to the time I headed to my next adventure, wherever that may be, life has been and will be always a risk, so I say live life like it's your last day on Earth. Make sure you fill your day with all the things you enjoy, from music to takeaways, from laughter to stupidity, from stupidity to seriousness. However, when you are trying to be serious, make sure you enjoy the fun elements when all's said and done.

During my lifetime, when someone says to me you can't do something because it is too much of a risk, I think to myself we are clearly built differently. My motto is risk it for a Club biscuit. I will give you an example. In 2012, I got a phone call from the NHS transport department, informing me that the transport I had organised for that day unfortunately wouldn't be coming. There had been crossed wires, and they were unable to take me to my appointment at Stanmore orthopaedic hospital in Middlesex. I was living in Worthing at the time. After the initial disappointment, I decided spontaneously to take myself to Stanmore under my own steam, having never been there on my tod before. I did not worry about this fact, as I had successfully completed a trip to Manchester some years before, so the journey to the hospital seemed like a journey to Tesco's to get some jam doughnuts! If you believe in your abilities to succeed, no matter how big a risk, you will undoubtedly succeed. However, if you do not take the risk then you will never find out the true extent of your risk-taking abilities. That might seem easy to say. However, if you've come from a family where all they want to do is protect you due to your condition, this is a lot harder to carry out. I suppose the way I have got round it is by self- determination and dedication in order to prove ultimately to myself "I can do this", whatever circumstances I find myself in. That is my attitude, and it has slowly but surely changed my family's perceptions about their vulnerable brother's/son's ability to live life and take risks.

The proof is in the pudding, as they say, and my chance to prove it came certainly to me when I got that call to say hospital transport was no longer able to collect me and take me to my appointment, as originally organised. Me being me, I took it upon myself to get to my destination, having never travelled to Middlesex and that part of London, on my own, and with no time to plan the trip. You can imagine that all sorts of thoughts and feelings were rushing through my head at a million miles an hour without stopping, just like the Eurostar from London to Paris. With my adrenalin pumping, off I went to the station to begin the journey into the unknown. When I got half way to the station, I rang Stanmore Hospital to tell them whereabouts I was and ask them if they would organise the community transport that takes patients from Stanmore railway station up to the hospital.

When I arrived at Worthing ticket-office, I decided to test whether they had ever been in a situation whereby they were to assist a frantically spontaneous disabled guy needing to know how to get to Stanmore at the drop of a hat.

"I don't care if you put me on a wing of an aeroplane, or, slightly safer, the underground, I just need to see my consultant at Stanmore hospital in Middlesex."

Several itineraries later, after breaking my wheels to get to the other side of the platform, I was boarding my connecting train into London. With a few minutes to spare, while waiting for the train to arrive, I had quickly scanned through the itinerary and thought 'Bloody hell! I should have just cancelled! I am never going to get there on time!'

It was twelve o'clock and my appointment was at four o'clock. I guessed the only thing I had on my side luckily was that the NHS and their appointments are always behind schedule.

On the train, reality began to hit me. How did I do what I just did? In approximately half an hour! If this doesn't boost my risk-taking capabilities, nothing will! I can do anything!

At this point in my memoir, I would like to make my book interactive and ask you, the reader, a question: **What do you consider to be a barrier?** You can find my email address at the end of the book. I look forward to some interesting comments and views.

Now the only thing to worry about was would the trains play ball and be on time. The answer to that was yes. Everything was going smoothly. **Until** some idiot decided to be inconsiderate and jumps on the line in front of the train. We had to board the next train which was only a few minutes behind on the next platform, so off I went. Nothing like a nice quiet train journey! Just as well that I like a bit of drama to make the day interesting. Once I was on my replacement train for the rest of the way, I studied the itinerary again. I knew exactly at what point I needed to get off the train.

To cut a long story short, I managed to be inside Stanmore station at twenty minutes to four. When I wheeled myself to the front entrance, I saw a vehicle with Patient Transport written on the side, so I found the nearest drop kerb, and loaded myself on their ramp.

"Are you going to Stanmore hospital?"

"Yes…and your name is?"

After all that, my appointment lasted five minutes and all went well. I know what you readers are thinking – you went all that way just for five minutes in front of Dr Spock?

You are right. I did go all that way for five minutes. However, on the way back I made up for it and took my time. I stopped off in Victoria Station to grab myself a double bacon cheese burger from Burger King. Yes, I did enjoy it. It was well deserved. And no, I didn't care that I looked like a bird's nest, full of crumbs!

Looking like a bird's nest was the last thing on my mind. I had completed successfully, whilst taking risks, a marathon, a journey that under normal circumstances I should have had patient transport to facilitate! I knew when I got back to my residence, my bird's nest would simply be cleaned up. At least people knew and saw I had earned myself a burger!

I would like to explain to you why I was able to do this risky journey at such short notice. The reason was that when I left Treloar, I had had to get a hotel for the night and then had travelled to Manchester with my friend, Frankie. Experiences like this made me trust my ability to carry out the most bizarre and risky tasks. When challenges like this crop up again, I will have no hesitancy in carrying them through, all because when you get put in tough situations it thankfully makes you stronger for the next occasion, and you come out safely the other side. So, I urge anyone facing tough situations not to shut down and give up. Always trust yourself and carry it through, because you will be a better person for it. Also, it will add to your stories and life experiences that one day you can pass on to your grand-children!

Surviving year one at Treloar College

I am quite surprised that I even survived my first year in college and didn't get excluded or expelled, because it only took someone to look at me the wrong way and I would be like a lion escaping from an enclosure – hunting for food and not stopping until it's been fed. I would end up in front of the student protection officer, giving me a warning about my behaviour and saying that if I carried on I would either seriously hurt someone or be told to leave college. After this specific meeting, I went away still full of anger, still not giving a crap. I would still be that lion hunting for more prey, were it not that one day I by luck bumped into my counsellor, Fiona, for the very first time at the college.

This would turn out to be the moment that my life and behaviour would change dramatically. It was when my intensive therapy started, and I found out that the cause of my anger was my mild PTSD which arose from my traumatic family circumstances. I would like to thank my counsellor, Fiona, and all the support staff for having faith in me and believing I could change. I would also like to thank my care manager, Trevor, for not giving up on me. But I also want to apologise for me being the most frequent visitor to his office. All of you have helped me come out the other side and I've been a better man for it ever since.

Now, because my mind is in the right place, it is as good a time as any to start explaining my side of the story.

Looking back on it, if I am completely 100% honest with myself, when I started college, my behaviour was actually what I would call normal for me. But over a period of three to six months, slowly I could see an ugly alien Adam coming towards me. In my opinion, the turning point for when the bad behaviour started to introduce itself was when I reached the grand old age of eighteen and was legally allowed to drink. That was the first problem.

But the second problem was seeing students regularly going home to their families and loved ones. Knowing I didn't have a home to go to that was sufficient for my needs, I am sure that was the major cause of the behaviour change. Both problems had occurred before the therapy started. These two components – the alcohol and watching students able to go home for the weekends on a regular basis when my unnecessary circumstances meant I wasn't able to – filled up my fuel tank very, very quickly, in all honesty, quicker than I ever imagined would be possible. Think of it as adding petrol to an already burning and out-of-control fire. That is what it was like inside my head at this time.

I relied on alcohol to be my inner counsellor. I felt numbness after around two or three Strongbows, which was what I drank every evening for the next year. During the day I didn't have my inner counsellor (the drink) to make me go numb. I wouldn't think about my non-existent home life, but my numbness was replaced by anger and outbursts of behaviour which in turn led me to not care about the consequences of my actions. This almost became a comfort and coping mechanism during the day, until seven o'clock came. Then I would get my daily dose of numbness so all of my anger and frustration during the days, weeks and months would go in an instant. It felt a big relief, like a massive weight being lifted off my shoulders. If I am honest with you, readers, I felt this became a bit of a routine, and something my alien self became very comfortable with.

Those of you who have turned, or have thought about turning, to alcohol, please, please don't. It will only escalate things until you are no longer in control of it. It will actually take control of you. I would like to take this opportunity, for those of you who may be struggling or indeed have struggled with alcohol, to say do not be ashamed to ask for professional help because when drink and negative emotion control you it's a very hard place to come back from. Sadly, it was too late for me. I was unable to get a grip on it. But thankfully, by my writing this piece, I would like to think I am saving at least one person and one life from drink taking control, just like a remote computer.

Of course, family is everything. I was denied seeing my family at this period. My people had been covering up reality because they thought they were protecting me when all they were actually doing was doing more damage than good. It was slowly tipping things upside down until I reached the point where I couldn't balance any more. I began to feel I would just have to go over the edge until I would hit the bottom when it would be all too late. I didn't get to see my brother or my family for a good half a year. This is the reality when you're covering up the truth. Next time when you phone me saying, "Could you stay at school this weekend, because I need to do something?" When in actual fact, the truth was that, except for me, everyone knew all along that I didn't actually have anywhere to go to, not even a roof over my head, stop and think. If you had just told me the truth, then I wouldn't have gone through some of my darkest moments as a teenager. Because of this situation, I felt very much alone battling my demons. Looking back at it now, it really wasn't a wise or intelligent choice of mine to go at it all alone and end up feeling isolated. My reasoning was: the person I trusted with my life (my brother) was now having to play the role of both parents, **as well as** being my brother, therefore I didn't want to add to his stresses and already huge responsibilities by telling him exactly what was going on in my nut. It's like getting a two for one offer in Iceland. In other words, I would rather that I alone went over the edge instead of both of us, unnecessarily destroying another family. But I have learned my lesson. Honesty is the best policy.

I am really grateful for receiving the support I clearly needed at such a time of turmoil from what I call the in-house rehab at Treloar College. In all honesty, it came just at the right time! After approximately six months to a year of me starting the college and receiving therapy, I started to see positive changes and, slowly but surely, we saw glimpses of the old Adam coming back. It was such a relief when, finally, I was heading into my second year of college (so, big boy time!) when I would now be seen as a role model to those first years coming through. Also, I was able finally to enjoy banter and jokes without going up the wall because of the alcohol talking nonsense. I found the relationship between myself and the booze became very distant, especially when after going to the doctor with a painful liver, he informed me my liver had become inflamed as a consequence of drinking too regularly. I must say this came as my wake-up call to stop drinking, to stop living a life of darkness and to wheel out and see the light. And there was plenty of it at the end of what had been a very, very, very long tunnel.

Chapter Nine

The other side

A goodnight

Through the whole of my second and third years at college I had nothing but success and achievement, which just a couple of months earlier I would never have dreamt to have been possible, let alone passing my independence transport programme that enabled me to be even more independent. I was able to leave college and start to plan, albeit only mentally, for the next phase of my destiny. Remembering this moment in my life, I would like to thank again all who were involved in my recovery from care staff and doctors all the way through to the social club bar staff for not serving me any more booze once I had reached my agreed limit for the night, which eventually put me off drinking the stuff regularly again. It's a fantastic feeling knowing I've got control of alcohol, and it's not controlling me. I am not planning for this to change any time soon or indeed at all. Thank you very much. Goodnight.

The morning after the night before

Good morning. I wonder what surprises there will be in my new lease of life. But I guess, before all that, it's time for my usual bacon roll for breakfast. Things get off to a great start when the bacon doesn't taste of rubber. For a change. Start as we mean to go on.

During my breakfast indulgence it suddenly occurred to me:

'I wonder if I could support students going through similar experiences that I've just wheeled out from.'

After twenty-five minutes to half an hour of deep thought, I decided for my own well-being and mental state, it probably wasn't the best timing, as I had just started my new lease of life and don't want to go backwards.

After breakfast, I found instead of relying on my old best friend, drink, I had started wearing my headphones listening to some of my favourite trance tracks, full of emotion and power to swing bad thoughts into exciting ones full of optimism and positive expectations. This is how I managed to keep positive and on track whilst not seeing my therapist.

This strategy was much healthier. For a start, I didn't get liver pains, just earache. My new-found form of music really began to show that I had come a long way in dealing with my emotions in situations where people were getting angry with me, as well as confrontations. Normally, with the old Adam, I would have given as good as I got, if not better. However, the new Adam just put the ear defenders (headphones) on and wheeled away. I found this was the best medicine to deal with any confrontational circumstances and people who thought they were Ronny and Reggie Kray.

"Do me a favour, turn your maturity level up and come back when you have done so and got brain cells the size of Bill Gates's."

After what I had previously been through, I was always going to find myself in tough situations. But I now began to deal with them by using my personality and my sense of humour. If you did this, certainly for me, it made tough situations into something that you could deal with. This now felt like a healthy routine instead of one that previously would see me go into decline. This routine became an unexpected comfort and I found my popularity soar through Treloar. That could only be a good thing, especially when it came to the weekends when the clubs were open! The way I was able to maintain this positive routine was as follows. Half an hour or so after breakfast in the morning and after dinner in the evening, I would just simply plug my tunes in. Then for the next half an hour, I would do as many laps as I could around the college, or sometimes the local village of Hollybourne, depending on the weather. Whilst doing my laps and with my tunes pumping, I would use the vocals and basslines to help put my emotions into order by making a checklist from one to ten.

Sorting out my own emotions like this assisted me to gauge the moods of others, because I would be able to scan my checklist, albeit silently, and pick out the right approach to deal with each individual. This checklist could differ depending on how I was feeling. If it had been a particularly emotional day for me, I would withdraw from interacting quite so much. This wasn't because I wanted to be unsociable. I just wanted to safeguard myself from a particular individual's emotions having a negative impact on me at that time. This is something I still practise to this day with practically everyone I meet.

It's like pushing buttons on a switchboard to connect you to and from different departments. I use the same method just to switch me to and from emotions, depending on whether I need to be serious or to relax and take the biscuit occasionally. It's a bit like being my own sound engineer playing with my internal emotions. I believe I have this great ability to switch my emotion knobs and faders up and down depending on the occasion and circumstance at the time. For instance, when I am with my friends, I turn down the maturity fader to almost zero but just leave a little gap just in case the conversation turns sour and gets serious. I can then immediately turn up the maturity fader without delay. Hence, the little gap I leave at the bottom of my emotional checklist. I do this with every single person I meet in my life. Another thing I also do is have a signal fader to help me gauge if the person I am conversing with is on my wavelength or not. If for any reason they are not, I make adjustments accordingly. The aim to end up on the same wavelength. Sometimes this is not possible, so I just accommodate the mood on a person-to-person, occasion-to-occasion, basis! Why all this trouble? It is how I have decided to get on with people. In my opinion, I get on with most people pretty well. I have the ability to make them feel at ease immediately and this helps, especially when it comes to my job as a sports coach. On the odd occasion, people can be quite eccentric and come at you out of the blue, so that I just can't fathom out their wavelength. Maybe they are only partially 'down-loaded' as yet. Maybe they are just not ready yet for release into the outside world. In other words, there will always be one person out of ten who I will not be able to get on with, no matter how many times I modify my emotional mixer.

These techniques started when my new lease of life began at college. They weren't just for college. I wanted to find out if the same technique could be managed when I eventually emerged from my college cocoon. So, really, Treloar became a test run to see if such an approach would work elsewhere. All these years later, I still use these same techniques and I'm still alive, so it can't be that bad. If you want to use these techniques, as far as I know they are seemingly exclusive to Adam. Having said that, nothing is impossible to teach. But why not work out your own techniques? One tip is buy a decent pair of headphones, so you can't hear if people are trying to distract you and divert you from putting your emotions into the best order for you as an individual.

At the end of the day, we are all wired differently. Because, let's face it, life would be pretty boring if we were all the same.

After I had completed several laps round the college I would go back to my daily routines as normal. This consisted of going back to my place of residence, doing what I needed to do, whilst being an idiot occasionally, some might say, all to get ready for my education. It was time for the so-called brainy activities to start. It's a good job I got on well with most of my form tutors, which made things that little bit easier and made the day go more quickly, instead of dragging on like the prime minister's press briefings. (**Please note**: do not be offended, if you are the prime minister or one of his fans).

It's amazing how time flies. I would normally walk in the classroom at nine a.m. if my mischievous side didn't engage my brain into talking to my circle of friends rather than being a goody-two-shoes and being on time for the brainy stuff. Personally, I preferred the practical side of my lessons, when I felt I learnt more. It sounds weird knowing I have only got the use of one hand to do practical tasks with, but heigh-ho, there we go. Such is college life. No sooner had I arrived, not sure whether it was on time or not, it was soon time for a bourbon biscuit. My break was spent chatting stuff that made no sense, eating bourbons and trying to get more free chocolate out of the vending machines. Sadly, I can count on my one good hand how much free chocolate fell out of the vending machines, so, Treloar, please don't worry, there was still plenty to go round for everyone else!

Once I had finished trying to knock over vending machines, if there was time, or if there was a lesson I didn't particularly like, I would choose this time to conveniently go for my comfort break. So, shout out to the Evans House care staff: if you ever wondered why you would see me at odd times, this was the reason...it just had to be done. I'm sorry! But at the same time, I'm not! After my own scheduled comfort break, it was then time to join the last ten or twenty minutes of the lesson before lunch. When I arrived considerably late, accidentally on purpose, I remember some tutors used to question where I was, which is understandable.

"I was being a good and responsible parent and dropping the kids off."

For those of you who don't know or use such phrases, this means sitting on the loo. This was my typical response if questioned by the teaching staff. If you are wondering, did my attitude change if very occasionally I was speaking to the vice-principal or principal? No, I just said it in a posher accent.

After five to ten minutes had passed, just enough time for my bourbons and free chocolate to digest, it was time for a typical rubbery lunch. I particularly used to do my best on a Wednesday, especially New Student Day, not to eat any chocolate because I knew, even if it was only once a month, the food would be decent. So, my routine was not to fill myself up with rubbish. After lunch, if it was a lesson I enjoyed, I would be at the lesson enthusiastic, feeling fantastic, ready to learn, like Eddie Hearne (boxing promoter). At four o'clock, the college day was coming to an end. This would normally have been a time alien Adam would be looking forward to my inner counsellor (alcohol), which was only a few hours away. However, due to my new routine, this was no longer the case. Instead, I would give my emotions something to look forward to, in the shape of **music**. That was only if I didn't have my sports club commitments.

This new routine took a while to get my head around. That was until I got what I call 'Little Adam' on board by helping him with what the right thing was to do. You may be wondering who Big Adam and Little Adam are. Big Adam is the physical specimen of Me, but Little Adam is also Me, only hiding somewhere inside instead. Little Adam always asks Big Adam for advice on what to do about things if unsure – and he is usually unsure. Big Adam always reassures Little Adam and tells him things will be OK.

"Don't worry. Be happy."

Weird? I can't be the only one on the planet who has a big and a little version of themselves. This is how I make some decisions in my life, combining the two Adams together to become one! People may think I'm talking to myself when I am wheeling down the road, alone. It is OK. I am not crazy. I am just running things past myself, whilst also reassuring Little Adam. I particularly have to reassure Little Adam when I'm in unexpected territory. This is also partly why I can keep a level head when other people are screaming. There are two of us for the price of one!

It's that time again

I was fast approaching the end of my second year at Treloar College, but I still felt I had a lot more to learn before I would leave Treloar for good and enter the real world. Before that, as I said previously, I worked very, very closely with physios, OTs, and care staff to start thinking about life after Treloar. Yes, I know what you are thinking. But, don't worry, I can be mature when I need to be. For the next year I would really focus on becoming as independent as I could, if not physically, definitely independent in the mind. For this to happen, if I was honest, given the first year and the first part of my second year, I would need to give myself a kick up the arse. Due to my new-found attitude, I was able to do this pretty much from the word go. I knew exactly what I wanted. I wasn't going to achieve my goals and dreams overnight. However, I knew I would eventually achieve them, if I fully committed myself for the next nine to ten months.

I found the process of becoming gradually independent quite a struggle at first, asking lots of questions, regularly getting confused, even wondering whether this independence game was really for me. To be honest, I did have some inner doubts. Little Adam was crying, and I was having strong doubts. They lasted about two months.

One morning I woke up with all the belief in the world that I would get through this and become as independent, physically and emotionally, as I possibly could. I don't know what it was, but a light bulb flashed on in my head and the rest was history. I just went to all the specialists whom I was working with, told them my revelations and goals and aspirations. I went from zero to hero – in my mind anyway. I managed to achieve staying in an independence training flat, where it skilled me up to such a level I began to do things that I myself didn't believe possible. When I managed to achieve something which on paper was impossible… when **that** happened, it gave me a feeling I cannot describe. If I were to explain my feelings at the time of these achievements, then I would say that it was like a blind man regaining his sight overnight, after many, many years of darkness.

A little helping hand

I would like to take you back to when you met alien Adam. Lots of people and professionals gave me the time and support I needed. Now I've come through and out the other side, I feel like it's time for me to give back time and support to people, and do my best instead of jumping in at the deep end. It has involved changing my emotional status and taking time to understand what people are going through or have gone through; in other words, doing all the things other people did for me when I needed it. Now the tables have turned. It's my turn to give back and observe/understand what emotions are really about. Are they about just how you feel or are they more about what you have come through? I guess, in a weirdly lucky way, I personally feel as though in my early adolescence I had been through almost every emotion known to man, and I am almost 100% sure as I go up life's ladder I will come across emotions that I never knew existed. But until I get to that point, who knows? All I can say is so far, so good.

Back in 2015, it took a very traumatic experience for me to educate myself in one of the trickiest vocations you can ever take a qualification in. I decided, due to that traumatic experience. (that is something I deal with later in this book) that if I wanted my bullet holes to heal, it would be a major positive achievement for me. But I needed to know a lot more about the healing process. I took a qualification in something I had been receiving since I was a little kid. Counselling is one of those subjects that, if you are going to master it, you have to do a course. You will find out about yourself and how you really deal with things, especially your personal emotions. I advise you to think long and hard about whether a counselling course is really for you. You have to take part responsibly. As I shockingly found out, sometimes when you are assisting someone to solve a problem, without knowing it, you can find get it badly wrong. What I got wrong in a practice session would have had a detrimental effect on the outcome. You can overdo the advice. I only found this out when I took the course, and we were covering the subject of self-awareness. It came to light during a session where I was asked to help one of the students with some hypothetical but realistic scenarios. Unknown to me at the time, instead of helping the situation I actually went the opposite way and became a hindrance. I overloaded the person with advice. Worrying. At the same time, fascinating!

As the course went on term by term, I found I was in a group of like-minded people, and I was someone who needed that emotional and human contact. Although the situations that are teased out can be tough, due to the nature of the course and the type of people it attracts, it gradually became easier to cope with. It's because you realise you are not the only one going through emotions that you have never yet faced up to. My personal motive for doing such a course was not only because I had had counselling for years. It was due to a traumatic experience I went through a couple of years previously. Some might say for them this would have been a step too far. My motto is you never know, so give it a go. I am so glad I did, because it contributed to my healing. I came to feel so much stronger and in control and self-aware after doing the course. It made me realise what triggers bad emotions, those very emotions that creep out from under the woodwork at the most inappropriate times. Thankfully, I can gauge when this is about to happen. I get a feeling of sadness running through my veins followed by a distinctive feeling that I know what to do, when to do it, and how to control it. This is where my saying comes from: 'do something that makes you happy!' I hope I have given you an insight into how things work for me, because some readers may pick up this book one day when they are down in the dumps and feel in need of some guidance about how to deal with feelings that are unfamiliar to them. Be happy, be lucky.

Never be embarrassed or ashamed of who you are. In life, sometimes we just need some help. If we try to fight all our battles alone, it can become like World War One and Two inside, every five minutes an air raid siren going off. So, if you are feeling as if you've got a World War mindset at the moment, please reach out to professionals, such as counsellors. This can be a hard step to take because, like I was, you may be in denial that you need any help. Once you have taken the first step, trust me, in certain circumstances it can be very painful. But remember, it is certainly worth it and will be beneficial to you in the long run. Having said that, don't expect the professional treatment to work like Harry Potter's wand. To get to the bottom of whatever your struggles may be, your therapy will take you on an emotional journey like no other. During the initial period, make sure you give yourself time and plenty of space to gather your thoughts. This strategy personally works for me. Another important point: when the therapy gets hard, do not give up. The counsellor cannot do the work for you. However, what he or she can do is give you tools to add to your tool box of life. Keep battling on, however hard and emotional you may get. Trust me, when I say there is light at the end of the tunnel. It may seem it is never ending but one day soon you will be at the end of the tunnel with the victory belts raised above your head. Then you can say, I've done it!

Chapter Ten

Systems

My relationship with the local authority

Let us look at the wonderful life living under local authorities, especially if your name is Adam. The job of a social worker can sometimes seem like a puppet show, as most of their decisions have already been made before your appointment. My job as a client is to undo the good work of their manager who has attached them on a puppet string.

'I always seem to need to tell the latest social worker the reality of life and, following that, the way I intend to live, whatever may arise. I appreciate that they work with a lot of vulnerable adults and people who can't communicate as effectively as I can, but that does not mean that every vulnerable person should be tarred with the same brush. We should be treated as individuals and be spoken to appropriately, according to our communication levels. It seems there is a lot of work to be done to change the way that intelligent individuals, such as myself and others, are assisted by authorities to live life how we need to, not just for their convenience. Whether you are disabled or not, we were put on this earth for a reason: to live life as freely as possible. Social workers need to understand that we are all humans, and they can't just make their own rules when it suits because, let's face it, that is the point of the law of the land, whether at national or local level. I don't know, maybe they are getting their job roles confused. All we can do is educate the already educated and see if we can change even the most professional perceptions!

I would like to mention a little bit about what it is like when you are a client on the front line trying to fight these uneducated educated people. This is for those of you who may not have been in direct contact with such professional people, and for those of you who are just starting out.

My first independent experience with my local authority was when I was approaching the age of sixteen. To be honest, I may have underestimated the challenge ahead of me which, I believe, is what led to my downfall and the reason why I am having such a fight nowadays.

When I was a kid, situations seemed easier as all the discussions took place on my behalf, so, as the individual under review, I was listening in the background until it was my turn to pick up my racquet and defend myself. Little did I know, it would turn into the longest game of badminton I've ever come across in my life. Still, to this day, I have yet to win one rally. My arms are aching.

I guess my life and freedom of choice is always worth fighting for. I just have to remember not to give up, even during the hardest of moments. Looking back, I wish I had done more research about how the system works and what the laws behind the system actually say, as I am sure if I had put the words *Disability Act* before every sentence that came out of my mouth, a bit like Dot Cotton reading the Bible so she can recite to you page for page, verse for verse, chapter for chapter... if I had done that with the authorities, my life may have turned a corner and I would have won the rally and possibly the game a long time ago.

So, my advice to those of you approaching the age of sixteen and wanting freedom and independence: do not just think it will be easy and over in five minutes. Because it won't. Do your homework. Because of my naivety as a sixteen-year-old, I feel I am still paying for it now. And yet at sixteen, I already had a clear pathway in my head. One of the first things Treloar, in particular the college, taught you from the outset was to start thinking about your long-term future now. At the time, I thought I was doing pretty well with all this, but indeed I was making a big mistake by taking something really important (my future) on without unearthing all the necessary evidence.

To be fair to Treloar, if it wasn't for their expertise, training, and patience, most of the students wouldn't be where they are today, especially those (me included) who were lucky enough to be given the chance for at least a week to face up to the practical realities of life, experiencing it for themselves. This happened when students went into their own flat or accommodation to see what life would be like on their own, without having the familiar safety net beneath them. The practical living programme was really useful, because they taught you skills relevant to what you would be doing in the community, such as meal planning, care planning (e.g. organising rotas), shift times etc. Without the facility to organise these aspects of my life, I believe I would not have the practical knowledge of being independent that I have now.

The difference between an ordinary community Occupational therapist and the ones we had at Treloar is that the community OTs do not go into any depth regarding independence such as cooking, cleaning etc. All the community OTs deal with is assisting you in getting the necessary equipment such as a bed, hoists, slings, toilet chairs and occasionally putting you on the scales to take your weight, for medical purposes. Treloar's specialist OTs do that but lots more. For example, when students are put into the independence training flats, the OTs are responsible for every aspect of your learning whilst in the flat, from cooking and preparing meals to setting bed time routines, exactly like you will have to sort out living in the community. The biggest difference is they are hands-on and get practical with their students, especially in working out if any assistive technology is needed to help students meet their needs when they are out on their own living in the community. This is why I believe Treloar have some of the most, if not **the** most, experienced and knowledgeable OTs/physios in the world.

Having said that, if I could turn back time and change one thing, that thing would be not to have any professionals in meetings with local authority social workers. Why? Because when you live independently in the community, you are on your own; you don't have a professional opinion, backed up with all the evidence, including the rights that are legally yours and written in the Disability Legislation, to support your case. The next best thing to becoming your own disability/equality expert would be preparation in a preliminary meeting with a fully informed Occupational therapist, before attending the meeting with the local authority social worker. After all, your social worker will have had a briefing meeting with his or her manager before going into the meeting with you. In other words, the OTs would still be involved, but only in an advisory capacity, preparing their disabled clients on the various Acts which, in my opinion, are vital for your case to run as smoothly as can be. If only I had thought of this idea when I was a student! That is not to say I can't start the ball rolling and put this suggestion to Treloar in person in order to help other students who may come up against the same difficulties as I have, especially if they are not privately funded. Hindsight is a funny thing, isn't it? So, I feel social workers lick their lips when young people leave establishments such as Treloar, as they know there will be no professionals to stop the local authorities bending the rules, so to speak.

The way I think things could and should improve when students are in their final year at school or college is for the professionals to design a new compulsory curriculum, preparing those students capable of living independently for when, unaccompanied by professional support, they face a meeting with a social worker. This is the way I think it should work: the head of occupational therapy should organise a weekly session before the end of the academic year specifically designed to teach students the rules and regulations in all the different Disability and Equality Acts, so that if students struggle to remember what's law and what's not, those lessons will be able to give them the tools necessary to fight their corner once they leave school or college and are on their own. All of the stuff covered in these lessons should be made into a booklet, so students can take them away ready for their social worker meetings in the future. I think this would be a fantastic opportunity for students to get the support that is necessary for the independent lives that they wish to lead, without spending the next however-many-years going around in circles and banging their head against brick walls.

Dealing with unforeseen circumstances

When I was a student and, dare I say, even before I heard anything about Treloar, I had always been a forward thinker and had the ability to act quickly as long as I felt in control. I didn't

99

feel the need for third parties assisting me to resolve a situation. But when I started my stint at Treloar, my ability to forward plan and take care of situations quickly improved quite dramatically. Although I already had this skill and thought I had nailed it before reaching Treloar, the teachers and professionals at Treloar School and College were the ones responsible for improving my skill even further, by adding more skills to the ones I already had. Skill learning at school and college is the secret behind getting stuff done quickly, maintaining self-control, and achieving high standards in life.

Speaking for myself nowadays, when a personal assistant leaves unexpectedly, this is when my skills really come to the foreground. You have to get these things right. What you will be put through is no one's fault, but when you face a situation without a personal assistant, it puts your life at a risk. This happened to me recently. So, off I went, thinking through lots of different scenarios and possibilities about how best to get myself out of this unforeseen situation. As a result of my calmness and ability to think on my bum, I was able to secure four interviews in the space of one day. What supports my skills-set is the fact that we have the internet and social media on our side. So, a day after finding myself without a personal assistant, I now have secured four interviews. The key is not to worry. Always have a plan A, B and C. A would be the best outcome, and C would be the path you would rather not go down if you can help it, but all the same you have to have it there just in case.

I have made this look pretty simple, but I can assure you it has taken me years to develop it to the extent I have, and I am still adding to it as we speak, so really, I have a lot more to learn. I love to learn. I believe I will still be learning even when God says, 'that's your lot!' I would like to stress to people that none of this comes naturally to me. But once I decided to embark on learning, then all things became possible. We do not start with a full set of skills and understanding. We have to acquire them. It is our many experiences, good and bad, that develop the many skills we need in our armoury so we can survive. This is all learnt. Michael Shumaker didn't just get in a Formula 1 car and start driving around the track at two hundred miles an hour. He had to go through a process of thoughts, feelings, skills, and body management to cope with the demands of travelling at such speeds (for example, G-force training!) I like to think I don't shy away from any challenge, regardless of pressure. I could be tremouring all over the place due to the pressure, but all I will have at the back of my mind is what the picture will look like when I have been successful.

The pressure is on

Pressure is one of those emotions in life we all react to differently. I am going to tell you the way I deal with pressure. For instance, if I put pressure on myself, I am absolutely shocking and can't deal with it. But I seem to be good when other people put pressure on me to carry out a task and achieve it in a specific time-frame. Ninety-nine times out of a hundred, I will achieve it. The reasons for this are my desire to prove people wrong, and the adrenaline I get whilst dealing with pressure head-on. This feeling alone helps me to forget the pressure is even on me, as I just focus and head for the finishing line so I can experience the satisfaction of a pressured challenge completed.

I have come to enjoy pressure and now see it as a necessary source of motivation. It drives me to improve my life circumstances. Without it, I would not be nearly so content with my life. I would be very interested to know how you, readers, deal with pressure. Maybe we could learn off each other! Don't be scared.

Sometimes, when you are in a meeting that is going to determine the next stage of your life, it is easy to crack under the pressure. You are sat in front of social workers, therapists, and other professionals and it is easy to make rash decisions without going through the thought process which focusses on the question: is this really the best outcome for me? This happens because, I feel, social workers' caseloads are so humongous. They will say and put things in such a way that they pressure clients to make rash decisions which turn out to benefit the professional and their work requirements, rather than the requirements and welfare of the client on their caseload. The quicker they get your case dealt with, the quicker they get to move on and be paid at the end of the month. I always bear in mind the meeting is about MY FUTURE, MY LIFE AND WHAT IS BEST FOR ME, not their work goal.

Social workers aren't really social workers anymore because of the pressure they are under. It's not only the financial problems that cause things to go wrong. It's the fact that social workers and their teams don't take into account what catastrophic impacts their decisions have on their clients. This needs to change but it won't, unless more clients like myself shout to the rooftops, so I am urging you if you are in similar circumstances, please step or wheel forth and give more of us a voice. A group declaring a problem is better than just one individual and the more of us with similar problems that get together, the more the authorities will do something about it. They will realise it's not that the clients are being annoying. It's actually an issue across the county, wherever that may be.

I know in this last section I have talked about social services in a negative light, however, there are a few social workers that do not give in to the pressures from above and will actually support you if you have a good case. They may not be able to change it but if you get a reaction from them that says "we believe your case is strong", I can only see that as a positive outcome, even if the final decision is not the outcome both the social worker and the client were hoping for. At least they have tried.

Time to change the system

When I was growing up, the world was indeed a nicer place to be in, but it seems that, as time has passed, not many people consider the difficulties in life for people with disabilities or related problems. For example, when I was ten years old, I could access the services that would support my disability so that I could lead a comfortable life, sitting in my wheelchair and moving forward. However, things turned sour when I reached the grand old age of eighteen. All those services that I once had either completely stopped or provided very, very limited access. I would like to stress my disability will never materially change, but it is getting worse simply because, since I became an adult, services to maintain my condition have been reduced. Now at nearly thirty years old, I have not had regular physio, to the extent I need it, for over ten years. As a result of this, I am left in pain on a daily basis and on pills that would send a horse to sleep, which is no way for a thirty-year-old, disabled or not, to live their life. I am meant to be in my prime, not on the decline, so in my opinion the government need to sort themselves out, stop being selfish and look after communities, especially the vulnerable in our community. Give us the services and support we need to live like anyone else.

People who know me, nine times out of ten say, "You are no different to anyone else. The only difference is your legs don't work."

Social workers don't say one thing and do the complete opposite. I was told I would be eligible for regular physio. However, when it came to the assessment, it turned out that I didn't meet the correct criteria to warrant the support I actually needed, and still do need. I think, regardless of race, disability, gender, sexuality, everyone is human, everyone has feelings and knows what is required. Why should a bit of paper and a bunch of animals (the managers of the social workers), who haven't even met the individuals they are discussing, make decisions on whether you qualify for support such as physiotherapy or transgender operations?

My bit of advice to Big Boy Boris is get rid of the paper and the pens, and start treating people on an individual-needs basis. Life is not designed on paper, so the decisions that are made shouldn't be either. In actual fact, some of the decisions you have made in your short tenure have had an impact like no one else could ever imagine. The sad thing is probably you don't even notice. Time to wake up, Big Boy Boris. Start living in reality, not pushing pens with your friends in their suits and their boots! I would like for you and your friends to live a day, just a day, in the shoes of someone with a complex disability. They maybe cannot speak, or cannot eat independently, or cannot hear, but still they have to deal with the impact of your (sometimes) rash decisions on top of the problems they already have got. For example, some of the decisions that have been made during an unexpected pandemic called Covid-19, not even a kid without qualifications, wearing a tracksuit, working in McDonalds would make. For example, putting covid-positive patients in care home settings! What? Making the vulnerable significantly more vulnerable, turning the lives of more families upside down! I just don't know what to say, apart from 'Sort it out or get out!'

My biggest wish is for our vulnerable people, just beginning their adventures, not to be interrupted by such stupidity. I would like to think that when I hit my box, I've lived through the worst, so that the people queuing behind me have an easier ride, a bit like the war generation have done for our generation! The sad thing is I fear for those behind me, because the way things are going it's only going to get worse, which frustrates me. But I guess that is the reality resulting from appalling leadership. One day this paragraph will end up on your doormat, Boris!

Chapter Eleven

Onward

Now, where were we?

The start of my third year at college was a very interesting moment because I did not know what my wonderful life experience had in store for me next. The feeling of anticipation was immense but something I took in my stride. Whatever faced me, I believed in my heart of hearts I could manage it, no problem. So, let's crack on. Whatever you may feel, let your mind be free. (*I believe it is really important to be able to prepare your mind by using these little mantras, certainly for me anyway. It builds my confidence.*) I was ready for anything coming out of the woodwork. Let the challenge begin!

The morning after the night before, it all seemed pretty straightforward, except that I was now a bigger fish heading towards shore, although I still had ten months of swimming left. Better get cracking with the energy bar. Thinking about it, ten months of learning doesn't seem a lot when you feel you still have more than your allocated time of learning to do. Never mind. This will be a test of my dedication and attitude, and drive for success. It was the first day of term, and breakfast time was concluding. The nerves started jangling, because I knew the next ten months could be life-changing. Luckily, I was in the right mindset to start the day on a positive note. After my usual bacon roll, I would normally mess around with friends, chatting absolute garbage about stuff that's not important, like, 'I wonder how many chocolates I can steal from the vending machine'. You'll be surprised, some may laugh, but I turned my maturity level up and cut out all the timewasting and trying to get the free chocolate. Time to be serious and get down to business.

I went back to my place of residence, sorted myself out and was one of the first students in college. My first mission was to make myself known officially to my year three tutor. With this in mind, and with the butterflies in my belly, that's exactly what I did. On approaching the classroom, all I heard was *Faithless Insomnia* coming from the room. Straightaway I thought 'This year is going to be amazingly sweet'. I knew the tutor and I had what seemed to be the same taste in music. Not bad for an old geezer, I must say! This put me at instant ease, certainly for the rest of the day, but it was too early to say for the rest of the year. Time would tell. The signs were good, so far, though.

Time brought me to the start of the official college day. I got there early to make a good impression for once! I noticed students that had begun college with me in the first year. I could hardly believe we were the ones heading out the door at the end of the year. How could this be possible? I asked myself. But that was the reality and I had the time to deal with it.

My third-year classmates started to arrive. This business was getting real. At least I was not the only one feeling these emotions. Our tutor called us to all come together, so he could outline the year's plans. This included academic work, obviously, but he also informed us that we would all be working very closely with OTs and the rest of the Treloar team, preparing us to move on, after Treloar! His words were powerful and for some people would leave a lasting impression. I am not embarrassed to say I was one of those.

"You get out what you put in. So, it is up to you what happens from this moment on!"

An important part of the third-year programme was something called Future Fest. This was something designed by Treloar for their third-year college students to go round different tables and look at new placements to go on to after college. I found this quite an emotional occasion. Not only did I know all those years of having Treloar and its services on my doorstep would be coming to an end soon, but I had also recently found out that the placement I had to fall back on in the holidays from college would be permanently closing, so all the upheaval would start up again. So, best get ready for Round Two. Ding! Ding!

Whilst feeling emotional and anxious as well as a lot of other things, I decided to head towards the Leonard Cheshire table, simply because their advertising looked appealing. I quickly realised it was in my home town of Worthing. That was so unexpected I had to do a double-take. I spent between five and ten minutes speaking to Marcus Richards, who was running my potential new placement. One thing that stood out and grabbed my attention was how independently-minded and set up they were. This meant I could still be as independent as possible, basically no different from what I was achieving at college. The only difference was the location and the smaller scale. If my current holiday placement had been remaining open, to be honest, there was no need for this situation to be happening. My mind was optimistic and made up. I knew where my next placement was going to be. On the other hand, I didn't want to be rude to the other services at the Future Fest, so I went for a browse and picked up a few freebies, such as pens and sweets. But I knew Fethneys was the one. Going, going, gone!

On that first day, in the third-year meeting with my tutor, I realised he was basically giving us a polite kick up the rear, to give us the motivation more than anything else! His words impressed me, influenced me, and starting the ball rolling towards my moving into the independence flat where I would fathom out my capabilities for living by myself, and whether this would be a realistic option for me. The independence flat was a tool designed to assist students on assessing whether being fully independent would be for them, or whether they would be better off in a supported placement where they could still be as independent as possible, but where the worry of not having enough support was cut out. This is a very crucial part of the work Treloar delivers to their students, identifying what support would be most appropriate for moving on at the end of college life.

This process was at an early stage for me. I was absolutely amazed at how much control I now had over my life, even though I was still a college student. God knows how I passed this independence assessment, but the fact is I did, and by the way it wasn't an easy process, by any means. The feeling of having your own keys for the first time in your life is actually one of the best feelings I have ever felt. For once, my disabilities weren't a factor. It was just like walking into an estate-agents, picking up the keys, and going off to live your dreams. Once I was through the door, the reality of what this would mean for the rest of my life really hit home. It was like when you have a flu jab and the all-of-a-sudden needle prick makes you alert. This is how I felt when I walked through the independence flat door.

Responsibilities? What are they?

I was soon in for a bit of a shock. My OT had a planning meeting with me. She outlined the expectations of the OTs and what would be required of me living in the independence training flat.

The meeting began simply enough. But then the responsibilities hit me in the face like a ton of bricks. For a while, I questioned my own self-belief!

"You're responsible for designing your own care rota for the house staff to come and deliver your care."

That was the shock. That had always been done for me. I reminded myself that this was training. If I had questions or concerns, I must not be anxious or worried about expressing them, because I believed that when you speak up you are showing true independence. It means you feel able to deal with it in the way that you need to. There was no point pretending I knew what I was doing. The people assessing me were responsible for my welfare and would see straight through any pretence. The best way to deal with situations you find yourself in which you don't know what you are doing is firstly to admit **to yourself** you don't have a scooby doo (clue) about it. Secondly, never be scared or ashamed to say **to the people training you**: "I don't have a clue what I am doing. Please can you repeat what you just said in a way I can relate to so that what you are asking of me I can carry out."

In my opinion, this is showing that I am independent upstairs even though I may not be downstairs!

The way I see it is that everyone is independent, but at the same time everyone is dependent. I mean to say, if it is decided that you need a more supportive living environment, that is also absolutely fine, because part of being independent is making choices that put your safety on the front line. If you believe it will be safer for you to be in such settings as supportive living, then, to be honest, in my eyes that is an independent choice well made.

Those who live in supportive living still are required to make independent decisions. Not everyone appreciates that. Often in life, people are so quick to judge before they actually know the truth and the details of what they are actually dealing with. Check the legislation. It is all there to read and think about.

With specialists or support workers or whoever may be assisting you. the important thing to remember is do not let them influence your decision-making, because at the end of the day you're the one going through life, so **you** have to be confident and comfortable with it. As long as you as an individual are happy that's all that matters. Individuals can give you advice. That does not mean you have to take it, especially if their advice would have a negative impact on the way that you feel you should live your life.

Thinking of myself for a moment. I believe people with disabilities should get more job opportunities in specialised supportive education, especially if half of the students or more are disabled, than is currently the case. If they were to have someone like myself, who is also disabled, who has been there and worn the tee-shirt, the students would have a member of staff that they could relate to, in terms of going through life having similar disabilities. If I was a person in supportive living, I would find this very beneficial and reassuring, because I would be working with someone who's been and done it before me. In my opinion, that is preferable to having a physio representing the supportive living clients.

I could even, as student support representative, from time to time agree with the physio for once and tell the student I'm supporting, "In this case, the professional is right because I know they are doing it for your own good and I know this for a fact because it personally helped me in the long run."

Travel assessment again

As my third and final year continued, I was gaining more and more independence skills, which were allowing me to really express how I felt and also what I could physically do. I was now able to book assistance to go on whichever public transport I chose, so that was a major improvement from where I had started off. Having freedom is probably the most surreal but best feeling in the world. Only one thing could top that: being told I was a lucky winner when my name was drawn out of a hat - I was going to Orlando, Florida, completely free for ten days. That was amazing!

As you are aware by now, to ensure the safety and welfare of all students during their time at the college, there was a high emphasis on every student being assessed to the highest standard of risk possible, even around the college grounds, never mind when they left the site. So, to be told by an OT that I would be eligible to go on a transport programme gave me an overwhelming feeling. It even affected the carers who were assisting me on a daily basis. They knew how much this opportunity meant to me, and also it meant less of an earache for them, as I would go on and on at them to let me off the leash.

"Come on. You can trust a bright lad like me. I went shopping for my mum, don't you know!"

I was often told I was a nuisance but, surprisingly to me, this was meant in a positive light, as everyone quickly understood that I would not stop giving them an earache until I got to do what I was capable of. It was just a matter of proving it on a book's worth of paper!

Maybe it was time to bang down my OT's office door and find out when the big day would be. So, that's exactly what I did.

"Hello, Adam, what would you like me to do for you today?"

"Please can you give me a date for when my transport programme assessment will commence?"

"Funny you should ask that. I have just had a cancellation

for tomorrow and, due to your excellent initiative, I would like to put you in. Would you like this slot?"

"That's a no-brainer. Of course, I would. What time do you need me?"

"Nine a.m. please."

"No problem. Absolutely extraordinary and a pleasure doing business with you!"

If I could walk, I would have been skipping all the way back to my residence. I had to do that journey in my own way, by pretending I was out in the community as a car driver. If other students were coming across my path, I would stop for them and give them right of way. I would like to point out the fact I wouldn't normally behave like this, but as I was in a good mood and full of excitement, I thought 'why not be generous for once?' When I went back to my place of residence, I had staff running towards me.

"Is everything OK? We have never seen and heard you like this before."

"That's because I've never been offered a transport programme that could change my life before!"

I celebrated the fact that I had a place on the transport programme list by … guess what? You guessed it! I ordered a Dominoes! But do me a favour. Don't tell my brother, Darren. Nonetheless, this Dominoes tasted extra special, so I could not deny my taste buds the opportunity.

"Sorry, Bruv. Needs must. This hearty take-away could make all the difference. Let's wait and see."

After the Dominoes, I wanted to have an early night, so I could be as fresh as a daisy for my assessment. I took a shower, went to bed and slept like an animal in hibernation. I must have slept well, because no sooner had they put me to bed than they were banging on the door.

"Wake up. It's seven o'clock!"

"Give me another five minutes!" I grumbled. "Pretty please. Thank you!"

After this time had passed, I was up and about, nervously ready to go, as I knew my life-changing day was just a few hours away! Who would have thought it? My trip down to the breakfast hall was the most nervous trip I've had as a student, at both school and college. I guess this tells you the enormity of my day ahead.

After breakfast, it was time for a nervous pee. I've got to say, ladies and gents, it was the quickest I've peed in a very long time. After this very quick pee experience, it was time to get my stuff together and bust a wheel to get to reception to meet the OT, aka the life changer. Like a typical professional (please take this in a jokey sense) she was ten minutes late, whereas I was half an hour early.

"Sorry, I'm late! I love your time-keeping skills. That's one box ticked straight away, and I do have to apologise – I got carried away at my desk!"

Where were we going for my assessment? Woking. On the way to the train station, my nerves were somewhat jangling. I just knew I had the capability to turn them into positive nerves.

Part of the assessment is to test students' capabilities and proactiveness, so basically the OTs do as little as possible. They only intervene if they feel the students are at risk. On my transport programme, I was instructed to book my own train travel assistance to board the train, and I had to do this as independently and safely as possible, which can be very daunting if you've not done this before. OTs are aware of this, so they don't say anything if it's a minor mistake due to nerves; for example, getting the wrong platform because, let's face it, everyone does it, assessment or no assessment. I would like to say, getting transport to and from Woking wasn't an issue. But part of an OT's job is they like to spring a surprise or two.

"You haven't been to the loo today. How would you manage this, if you were out by ourself?

Oh dear. You've got me here! I will have to think of something.

"I had a very big, nervous wee before setting off, so I'm fine until we arrive back to college. But, to answer your question in more detail, I would quite like to try convenes, if at all possible."

"This is something we can of course discuss when debriefing your assessment."

Then she said one of the most satisfying things I have ever heard.

"It is now up to you, where you go. You have an hour and we'll meet you back at the clocktower. But we will still be keeping an eye from a distance."

At this point I was in my element. I first went to HMV and bought the latest CD I wanted. Afterwards I went to my favourite restaurant, Burger King, and ordered myself a Double Bacon Whopper meal.

Me being me, I decided, rather than struggle to eat and look like I belong in a zoo, it would be easier and cleaner to get one of the Burger King assistants to help me consume my burger. During this process, I could see the OT out of the corner of my eye with somewhat of a surprised look on her face. As I was already half way through, I just carried on and acted oblivious whilst at the same time, knowing this probably wasn't the brightest idea I have ever had: getting a strange Burger King assistant to feed me my burger would probably get me a mark down due to health and safety concerns.

I had to be at the meeting point by three o'clock. It was now half past two, so I had half an hour to do some browsing or window shopping, but I chose not to. Instead, I went to get a pick n' mix from Wilkinson's, went back to the meeting place with fifteen minutes to spare, and sat in a reclined position scoffing the lot, by which time the OT and her clipboard were in front of me, ready to head back to the station and begin the process of returning to college. The way back was pretty similar, and as straightforward as the outward journey. No issues, as far as I knew. Booking and boarding the train all went according to plan, so much so that we arrived back at college sooner than expected, which meant one thing. More time to debrief my assessment.

So, it was down to the office we went. We had a half hour debrief. The first thing that she brought to my attention was the amount of confidence I had. She was amazed that I made no errors getting the train to and from Woking, which I could only take as a positive. Then she moved on to whether she had any concerns that I was putting myself in danger. I was absolutely right – I did get marked down for the Burger King assistant feeding me my burger, although she did admire the fact that I had the balls to ask them for assistance, but couldn't agree it was the safest thing to do. Their reasoning was the fact the assistant didn't know if my disability impacted on my ability to eat, therefore they could have caused me to choke. Apart from that, it was plain sailing. She admired my ability to carry out my assessment to the extent I did, knowing I was being observed in a completely new set of surroundings.

What I thought was impossible at the beginning of my journey has just been made possible. I am now a fully-fledged green light student. Hard work definitely pays off, so, time to

116

celebrate. What better way to celebrate than to go down to Alton train station and book a train for a day trip to London? Some might say 'nothing like taking advantage of your new green light assessment'. I just say 'why not take full advantage and make the most of what you've got before it's gone!'

I stayed true to my mantra and made the most of everything that my third year at college had in store for me, some of which were amazing memories, especially when myself and a friend went exploring London for the day. We both ended up in the middle of nowhere. Maybe this was because we had no longer a route to stick to, provided by the OTs. Nevertheless, we had an awesome day, and arrived back at college just in time for an overcooked dinner.

My favourite memory of the entire three years at college was when I turned eighteen, and all my friends brought me a shot, or rather a series of shots. After each one, I had to spin round ten times, then drink another and repeat. I didn't just lose the ability to drive my chair, I also became somewhat weird and lost all control of my limbs, worse than normal. It was like I had too much baclofen all at once. For those of you who don't know, baclofen is a medication used to relax muscle tone. I felt like Dwayne Johnson on steroids. Although it was rather fun, so not complaining.

In the morning I met my house manager, Trevor.

"I hope you've got lots of money."

"Why's that, Trev?"

"Because of your actions last night".

As a result of me losing all control and half of my stomach contents due to vomiting, which may have had something to do with my alcohol intake that night (not sure!), I was fined £50 by the college. They said I had been irresponsible and out of control, and took up too much staff time. That was one expensive night, but who cares? It was my eighteenth birthday! If there was ever a lesson to be learnt, that lesson was do not consume ten shots of all different kinds, then spin round full speed in an electric wheelchair. Just not a good idea, especially on your bank account... and when your brother threatens power of attorney over a Dominoes pizza! I wonder what he would say over a fine for being overindulgent and irresponsible due to alcohol. I think that's all of my three chances blown at once. Bye-bye independence!

Future care placement

Whilst I had been living with my brother, we had discussed, as a family, what alternative placements for my holidays from college would be suitable. As you know, the first placement was absolutely diabolical and I wouldn't allow my dog (if I had one) to stay there! Looking on the brighter side, the second placement, however, was really home-from-home. That was the best way to describe it. It suited my family and I down to the ground. What was also most surprising was that they knew I had a college placement, so would only be home with them at the end of term. Extraordinarily, they kept my room open for me to come back to in the holiday times. Not only was it home-from-home, it had a very intimate staff team, which very quickly became a second family.

I had a particularly good bond, it surprises me to say, with the manager of the home. I know what you are all thinking: 'Oh, my God! Really? Adam getting on with a manager!' But yes, this is a rarity but true. The main thing I liked about Future Care was that we all had our own room, which was personalised exactly to our tastes. Just to give you an idea, the manager, Ian, was very talented. He managed to hand paint, almost identically, the Chelsea FC logo onto my bedroom wall. To me, and for many others, for a manager of any home to do this is practically unheard of. For that I would like to say Ian, you are a top geezer! The home had all four residents' very best interests at heart. If ever I felt down about previous or existing issues, I would talk to the manager for hours on end and, importantly, feel that I was being understood.

From what I can recollect, the longest conversation we ever had was after I got very frustrated. After that, Ian had to buy a new door, as I decided to redesign it and put a footplate-shaped hole in the bottom. Although it didn't help the door or the care home budget, it didn't half help my boiling point level! The situation had subsided after a few hours, so Ian decided to go to the local fish and chip shop and buy everyone our dinner for the evening. If I was a manager and had a resident put a hole through my door, all that my residents would have got is bread and water, not a jumbo saveloy and chips. I remember our conversation lasting until about two a.m., just talking, and him helping me think of better ways to manage my frustrations, rather than sending the bill through the roof on buying new doors.

During our conversation, I remember Ian explaining a very important fact about cerebral palsy. This was when people with the condition get emotional, whether it be happiness, sadness or anger. Because of the condition, these emotions are actually taken to the extreme. If you are wondering how extreme, just reread the bit where Ian had to buy a new door! I have the utmost respect even to this day for him and all the staff, and what they did for each and every one of us. Possibly, one of the best ever placements I have ever resided in. That's saying something for

West Sussex. Credit to you all. And thank you, Daz (my brother), for yet again doing the social worker's job for them in finding me the ideal placement. I still can't quite believe that Future Care had to suddenly close for reasons out of everyone's control. Such sad news for the community.

Transition

After many years of being taught independence of a different kind, it was now time for me to graduate from Treloar before starting a new chapter in my life. However, this didn't come without its fair share of challenges. It's not just a case of lifting up boxes, moving them from one place to another. It felt like I was fighting for my life, the most pressure that I had ever experienced as a young adult. However, I was aware that if I used my independence training to the maximum, I would be absolutely fine. I was completely aware of what was going on and who was involved. I also knew I would be hunky-dory, as I had one of the best human beings on this planet in my corner, my big brother Darren, supporting me every step of the way whilst still encouraging me to be as independently minded as possible, especially through the ups and downs.

A 'down' for me to confront became apparent when Social Services didn't have anything in place for me on leaving Treloar at the end of term. I was due to leave Treloar and depart for a placement millions of miles away but it wasn't yet ready due to the lack of bed space available.

I was told by Social Services, "Don't panic. We will get something short-term in place for you."

I was not holding out much hope as my leaving date was drawing ever closer with still no plan in place. I decided to safeguard myself, because it was looking increasingly likely the Social Services plan wouldn't materialise. It was fair to say time wasn't on my side on this particular occasion in my life. What an opportunity to start maximising my independence training!

On the Thursday night before I was due to leave, knowing there was still nothing organised, I used my initiative. I went down to the local hotel and booked myself a one-night stay at the White Hart hotel opposite the college, so at least I knew I wasn't going to be on the streets. On the morning that my placement at Vitalise came available, I left the hotel bright and breezy, went to the local train station and travelled across the country on my own to my new placement where I would spend the next six to eight weeks before the next move.

On reflection, as a disabled person, I now recognise I created an impossible situation when I stayed at the White Hart hotel. I am not afraid to say that, even at the time, in order to make the impossible possible, I knew I would have to do something quite simply out of the ordinary and out of my comfort zone. I set about trying to convince the hotel to do my care needs. I had to do get people I had never met before to provide my personal care, knowing the potential danger I was putting myself and the hotel in. As you can imagine, the hotel's reaction was not positive, which I completely understood as I felt the same way. But I just had to make the best out of a bad bunch of apples. If it wasn't for the hotel stepping up, I would have been in dire straits because of the so-called social care system. Because they did not put a plan in place, this was the next best thing. Treloar had closed for the summer, so there was no going back to them. What were my feelings on this particularly stressful occasion? I felt I may as well have been my own social worker, as I was basically doing their job for them. As the saying goes, if you want a job done well, do it yourself. I would also like to point out this: how can the social care system call me a vulnerable adult when they have put me in the most vulnerable of situations?

My fears were not yet over, as I still had to get a train cross-country to my placement, somewhere I had never travelled to, especially not on my own. It was, for me, one of the most daunting and challenging moments ever. Despite this, I knew I had to get to my placement in Manchester in one piece, so all my forward planning and energy went into making it a successful and safe trip. I am pleased to announce I lived to tell the tale.

If you are starting out on your independence journey, this next episode is a good one for you. I would like to share with you how I was able to accomplish my mission. Time was of the essence. A lot of what I organised was off the cuff. It consisted of advanced planning, days before the event. It's a marvellous idea to have an A to B plan, not A, B and C plans, as you want the plan to go smoothly from A to B. In order to do this, have a photographic image of what you want your endgame to look like. Then you are better placed to minimise the risk of failure. The reason I say have a photographic image is because the image helps when you are trying to explain situations or scenarios to the people assisting you to achieve your A to B plan. For instance, if a vital bit of your assistance is to have an assistance ramp to board a train for your journey, make sure this is included in your photographic image when you are instructing the assisted travel team, so that there is no confusion. Give them direct, clear instructions, such as the time of the train you want to get, whether you need help with luggage or boarding the train, and if you need a taxi at the other end to take you to your final destination. All this stuff was a key to my successful journey across the country. As well as doing your job, always make sure you get the people assisting you to do their job. I guess there is an element of trust in whoever is helping you, as you have to hope they will act upon your requests, which is not always guaranteed, of course. However, the clearer your instructions, the more satisfactorily your requests will be dealt with.

Chapter Twelve

Influences

The part of life I think is funny

When I was growing up, I got used to it. I thought it was funny. Now I am an adult, I still have to put up with it. It happens frequently when I am out in public. It occurs most frequently with one sector of the population: the elderly (unless the old person has lived with or worked with people with physical disabilities and other conditions). Sometimes in life, we come to a stage where we get used to something, which makes you laugh on a consistent basis. Anyway, I love educating our elders because they have done so much for the country I've grown up in. I find it fascinating to watch their reactions when I open my mouth and their perception and opinion of me changes quite dramatically.

Here is an example of what I mean.

"You, young boy, shouldn't be out on your own. You should be with the people responsible for looking after you!"

"Thank you for your concern, my love, but it is not my legs that speak, it's my vocal cords, and as far as I can see and hear there's no problem with those. And, did you know, I am a Level 1 and 2 qualified sports coach, so I do believe I know the difference between a red and green man on traffic lights."

Pause for thought.

"Ok, dear, here's some wine gums…" and she pulled out

some Rowntrees. "Have these while you're out on your journey. Have a lovely day."

I also find it hilarious that, on the occasions I am out in the community with support staff, a member of the public's automatic response is to talk to my assistants rather than myself. A few years ago now, I was in that situation where a cashier in a shop was scanning my shopping whilst speaking to my assistant and asking questions that should have been asked to me.

I would normally pipe up and say, "I can talk, you know. I am not a robot."

But on this occasion, I decided to have some fun and sat there and watched this episode of Supermarket Sweep! Only at the end, when my carer was packing the last few items into the bag, did I pipe up.

"Hello, how are you today? Have a good one."

The cashier's face was a picture. Pity I didn't photograph it for my album.

Now it is time to tell you about my all-time favourite. This was when I was working on behalf of a company that focussed on disability awareness and changing perceptions of young people in schools, something I very much enjoyed and would go back to in a heartbeat! On this one day, I was doing a talk for disability awareness. It is a routine of mine to have a Q and A with the school pupils. I am used to weird questions, reactions and answers.

"Are you related to Danny Dyer because you sound like a gangster and you wear a sovereign ring?"

First of all, I was stunned into silence. Hard to imagine, I know. A silent Adam. Put me in front of a bunch of kids who don't give a crap what they say to whom, not even to a special case like myself. But I wasn't silent for long:

"You're a legend! Sadly, no, I am not related to Danny Dyer. Cheers for the compliment. Top man!"

Another time I was working in a school, again doing a Q and A, and I got the kids to guess what TV programmes I watch. A girl put her hand up and said, "You watch Tricia and the Jeremy Kyle show."

"Yes, occasionally," I said, "but what makes you say and that?"

"Because you wear tracksuit bottoms, even on a special occasion like visiting our school."

Insulted? Me?

"You kids amaze me. I just think you are absolutely brilliant. I am glad you like my choice of work clothing."

How best to educate people who are ignorant about disability? This is not done by Effing and Blinding. I never put anyone down. Let them say whatever's on their minds. I take a humorous approach, so that it is OK, nothing to be scared about or embarrassed by. The aim is to make their ignorance disappear, and you begin to see them relax and, by the end of the conversation, what started as quite abrupt or awkward ends calmly, in a relaxed way. The trick is to have patience. Try to understand and put yourself in the ignorant person's shoes. Think to yourself, 'I might be the very first disabled guy they have communicated with.' It is only ignorance you are dealing with. No need to make them feel bad.

The reason I wanted to share with you how I deal with ignorant people is because I get a lot of disabled people and their carers not necessarily complaining but having a gripe at the fact people are so ignorant. I feel it is not just up to the ignorant person themselves to overcome their ignorance, it is also up us all to take the responsibility to change people if we do not like their individual perceptions or attitudes.

Parents introducing their children to personal finance

To parents or legal guardians who have a young adult with disabilities (or even without) that has independent access to their own finances – if you find their spending is spiralling out of control, my advice is to put in carefully chosen rules and guidelines. Make it clear that you would, if need be, activate Power of Attorney. When all else fails, that works a treat! Sometimes you have to be cruel to be kind and have your son or daughter's best interests at heart. I know from experience (me as a young adult) that if you allow the situation to get too out of control, you will then spend a considerable amount of time playing catch-up, having frank and uncomfortable conversations about something that is simply down to a lack of maturity. The quicker you nip things in the bud, before they reach the no-turning back age of 18, when the parents' or guardians' control by law over your son or daughter becomes very limited, the better.

Young people when taking on responsibility for their own finances

Hi, peeps! I just want to give you some friendly advice about your finances. For those of you who are at the age where you have access to your own money by law (that is, from the age of 16) with your parents' guidance and say-so, this is not a time for you to start thinking that you're Bill Gates and can spend money like water. What started as a privilege could end up being a horrific nightmare. So always try to be responsible with the money received in your accounts, either from your parents or the state. Take this from someone who's been there and worn your shoes and your tee-shirt and spent in excess of £80 at its worst on take-aways and unnecessary materials such as CDs, lads' mags...the list goes on. So, I am urging you to please be very, very sensible and spend your money wisely, as you never know what the future holds. What you've spent on the unnecessary good stuff you might need in an emergency, and you will find you simply haven't got it. So please be safe. Never give your account details to anyone you don't know. Furthermore, if you get a phone call and they say it's the bank, immediately put the phone down, as the bank will never ring you – this is a scam.

Advice to the rest of humanity

Read the above!

Advice to parents: managing expectations and problem-solving

My advice to any parents who have a young adult with a disability, whether it be a physical disability or a learning difficulty, is to approach situations with an open mind; as the old saying goes, *expect the unexpected*. The reason I say this is because I have been caught out on a few occasions, thinking people in authority are going to go along with my plan. As a young adult, you dream your dreams and you make plans and it seems OK until you pluck up the courage to make an appointment with someone you think can help you. As soon as you get into your appointment and you have told them your plans, they try their very best to throw them under the bus! The example I am going to give illustrates the difference between children's services and adult services. When you are a child, there is a lot

128

more flexibility within the system – for example, you get more services, such as easier access to funding for wheelchairs and mobility.

At the age of twenty, I fancied playing wheelchair football but didn't have the right wheelchair to play. I decided, me being me, I would chance my arm and go down to a local garage and ask them to design something for me to be able to play the game. When I decided to do this, several people had their doubts whether I would pull this marathon off. As previously stated, *where there's a wheel there's a way.* Within four weeks, my marathon came together like glue. In October 2010, I was playing wheelchair football for Brighton and Hove Albion, aka the Seagulls. In my opinion, perseverance is key.

Don't be scared.

Never be scared to assist your child's/adult's journey through life, and sometimes you just have to grit your teeth, even when you do not want them to do something. Take that leap of faith, and let your offspring have experiences and take risks and learn to do things with a degree of independence, whether you think it is safe for them or not. In my personal opinion, taking a risk or two is part and parcel of growing up, whether in a wheelchair or not. After all, it is the world that makes us disabled and therefore it is the world that has to be accepting and have room for error. My advice is *risk it for a biscuit.*

Difficult situations.

Fortunately, or unfortunately, depending on how you choose to look at things, having a disability throws objects of all different shapes and sizes in all different directions under your chariot, especially when having the social care system involved in your life. One personal situation I can give you is when I was residing at a care home in Worthing called Fethneys. I was planning to move in to a bungalow with my best friend at the time, Harry Glas. Harry and myself were as incredibly excited as kids at Christmas about our planned adventure as we headed into our transition meetings with social workers, only to find out that our plan was considered too costly and unsafe! This left us feeling very demoralised and, in a sense, worthless, as if we were just a figure or a number on their database. Therefore, I expressed my displeasure and told everyone to get out the damned room and leave me alone! Things got a bit heated due to the passion we both had developed striving for independence. Unfortunately, our plan was very quickly pulled from underneath our wheels. It didn't work out, but the best advice I can give you is always fight for what you believe in as long as the goal is realistic and achievable.

Musical influences

One of my biggest passions is music. People say they can't live a day without some sort of music, whether it be a brass band or techno. I completely agree. I don't just listen to music, music has a meaning in my life. Music to me is like a personal counsellor. It may sound strange, but it's music I have to thank for guiding me to be the person I am today. I feel my particular genre of dance music brings out my personality without any verbal communication at all! When they hear my music, most people know me before they see me. The type of music I listen to has a lot of energy and is very upbeat, and that more or less is true of my personality. I have proof of this. When I was doing a disability awareness talk in a school, I asked a pupil if she could guess what kind of music I was into. Sure enough, to my amazement she guessed dance music straightaway. Yes, I know you are all desperate to know where my love of dance music came from and the inspirations behind it! Big Brother (not the TV programme, my actual big brother). I first heard a dance track at the age of six, as I used to share a bedroom with my big brother Darren in our three-storey house. I remember this like it was yesterday, lying on his bed, stretched out so relaxed, not even a bomb could make me jump, listening to the words and music of *I Can't Get No Sleep* by the legends Faithless. I fell in love from that moment, living and breathing every beat and melody. As soon as the music entered my ear drums, I would go into another world far, far from reality. The music gave me the chance to think about what my life could and would turn out to be, all without having people voice their opinions and pass their judgements. I would allow the music to take control of the emotional side of my brain and go with the flow and tempo of the mix, which pretty much describes the way I dealt with and still do deal with my emotions. Personally, I feel this is the safest way for me to deal with any unfamiliar emotional situations and circumstances. I say to my readers: give it a go, as it may bring the ever-increasing crime rate down just a tad! Maybe music really is the answer.

Most weekends, my brother would play *90s Trance and Techno* whilst getting ready to go to an old night club, commonly known as Stearns. I would always be present, not because I wanted to chat to my brother, I just wanted to listen to the music. It was my time to relate to what I have grown to love. Then the time would come for my brother to go to the club without me. Little did he know that, when his back was turned, I used to ask my mum to sit me in my therapy chair to help with my balance, position it alongside the stereo, move one of the many boxes of CDs where I could reach them independently, and then I would start to play and listen to my much-loved dance music to my heart's content, not forgetting to occasionally turn down the volume so I could check if Darren was coming up the stairs. This was because he treated all his CDs and cassette tapes like they were his babies. He didn't like anyone touching or playing with them, especially someone with a disability and limited hand movement. As I'm sure you know, CDs and cassettes are very delicate and easily scratched and ripped. My secret intrusion into my brother's precious music tapes and cassettes continued until one day when I very unfortunately accidentally ripped one of the rarest cassette tapes that my brother owned. My first thought was 'Oh shit! What could the matter be?' I opened the tape deck only to find the rare tape chewed to buggery. That was a shame, but I was more concerned about my brother's emotional side of the brain! When he found out what I had done, he would be more King Kong than happy bunny. But I guess you do silly things when you are in love with something!

Chapter Thirteen

Fethneys

I have made it

After my various trips back and forth to Manchester, Nottingham and Southport, it was finally time to reach the final destination: my home town, Worthing. Here, I would spend the next four years, before reaching my ultimate goal and dream of having my own set of keys and flat. But now, my very first physical experience of Fethneys! For those of you who don't know, Fethneys is a transitional care home in the centre of Worthing, for young adults mainly with physical disabilities. The home's focus is to build on the independence skills gained already by the individual residents, and to give them that extra boost before living completely or partially independently. In other words, it is a half-way house, or, as I like to call it, university without the study, just the party life! That is, if you were highly skilled in the first instance, like I was! Fethneys is an initiative of Leonard Cheshire Disability, the main focus of which is physical disabilities. The reason for the university analogy is the age range from eighteen – twenty-five years. The other reasons for my 'uni' analogy you will find out in due course.

During several months waiting for a bed to become available at Fethneys, I was stuck in an old people's home. So, when I got my starting date at Fethneys, it felt like I had had been reborn. I was filled with optimism and enthusiasm. I couldn't wait, although I had learned to enjoy watching the Antiques Roadshow on a loop and finding out what many generations sacrificed to give us the life we've got now! I was in bed one evening when I got a rather heavy knock on the door. The door opened and it was a female carer with a man's knock, which I found inspiring. She came with fantastic news.

"We have a moving-out date so you can start your new placement. They now have a bed available."

Trust me when I say I was elated. If I could have jumped out of the window, stood on a rooftop and shouted, "Bring It On", then I would have done so.

With three days to go, I was starting to pack what I had unboxed which, to be honest, was only a handful of items. I put them away and one of the staff members said to me, "This the happiest I have seen you in seven weeks."

"Well, it's funny that, because it's true."

That evening, I decided to escape the confines of old people to go and see the fireworks on the coast road by Worthing Pier. The powers-that-be weren't happy, but there was nothing they could do as I didn't need to ask them for their consent. Happy days, I guess! After the fireworks, I went and got a takeaway, which I enjoyed so much because the food I had been consuming recently tasted years out of date. It was nice to have a fresh but unhealthy KFC. It was the kind of cooked chicken I'd known all my life. After this indulgence, it was getting on for approximately eleven o'clock in the evening, so I thought it was probably best to start heading back before the authorities spent a fortune and sent out a police helicopter to look for me! On my way back to my accommodation, I noticed lots of people giving me weird looks. I found out why when I was approaching the care home's driveway. They were actually already looking for me. Oh well, I guess my independence training was serving its purpose. I still had one bit of chicken I was munching without a care in the world whilst approaching the home. But concern about my whereabouts was all around. Everyone was asking me my name. I felt like Katie Price getting hounded by the media. It seemed, if only for half an hour, I was the most in demand disabled youngster in Worthing. Eventually the senior nurse came out and said, "Are you Adam?"

"No, you are mistaking me for my twin," I jokingly replied.

To be fair, they took this pretty well, considering the circumstances of search parties out looking for me. Once they had figured out that I indeed didn't have a twin, panic buttons were no longer pressed, and I was able to enjoy a Nesquick milkshake before getting into bed.

With only a day to go, I thought I would use my vast training and prepare for my move. So, I went shopping to buy stuff for my new Fethneys adventure! After my shopping trip, I thought I'd spend the rest of the day in the social areas of my current home just to get to know, after my young lease of life has departed, what it would actually be like when I need to be a genuine resident of an old people's home. I decided to imitate what the old folk did and follow the home's daily routines as if I was living there permanently. I have never had such a laugh. Everything they did I found highly amusing. For instance, seeing every single resident drinking from a cup and saucer with their pinkies in the air all at once. Incredible sight! I also saw some of the most wicked dominoes and Jenga players I had ever seen. But the best time of the day is when they are all eating dinner together and they start arguing over who's having the biggest bit of bread to go with their rather small cup of soup. Soon after the scheduled dinnertime, all the residents were getting ready for bed. I went to my room to listen to the latest Tiesto album. I imagine the old people wheeling down the corridors or in their own rooms having a rave-up! By this point it was close to the cut-off point for loud music, eleven o'clock-ish. I decided to turn Tiesto off and get into bed for what would be my final night's sleep for a long time in an old people's home!

It was the quickest of night sleeps. In fact, it was like waking up after being anaesthetised. It was that quick. The day had finally arrived for me to press play, once again, on my life adventure. MOVING DAY!

The day of my move was actually the earliest I had got up in seven weeks, as I could not wait to be set free. I remember my social worker at the time met me out the front of the care home and walked alongside me to Fethneys to see if I would settle into my new surroundings OK!

"There's no need for your company but thank you anyway. You are more than welcome. Just tag along if you want."

When we arrived, I remember heading into the kitchen area where I was met by Sally and her daughter. Sally was cooking the evening meal for everyone. Whilst dinner was busily being prepared, I decided to go and check out my new room but my first mission was to work out the lift, so I didn't get the buttons back to front and end up in the basement. Luckily the lift didn't extend to the basement. I finally landed on the top floor of Fethneys. I was greeted with a creak, as soon as I wheeled along the floor. My first thought was 'Have they put me in an old nunnery or something?'

Anyway, I continued round to my new humble abode, which soon became very personalised, I can tell you. It was a surprisingly big room, and so I thought I could do quite a lot to make it mine! Overall, not a bad amount of space to live in.

After surveying my surroundings, the smell of dinner was getting stronger and stronger. I guessed it was time for grub. I got back in the TARDIS (lift) and pressed the down arrow, then it politely informed me that I was going to ground level, where I was welcomed by the very outgoing Collette on the way to the dining area to experience, for the first time, a cooked meal made freshly by Sally.

"This food isn't half bad, you know. Sally, your cooking reminds me of my nan's. Great job!"

If I was to describe my first week to a month of my Fethneys placement, I would describe it as a jigsaw piece slotting into place. This was, of course, because it was a good overall set up, but I think even more to do with how often I had changed placement. I had just gotten used to the feeling of moving around, so I did not find it a challenge to move in and start mingling. Also, I felt it was similar to Treloar, albeit on a smaller scale, and without any of the lesson commitments, which to begin with I found weird. How each day was decided depended on how proactive and independent I wanted to be. In other words, it would only be boring if I allowed myself the opportunity to get bored.

In fact, I soon discovered there were plenty of opportunities to improve my initiative skills, and that meant I would very rarely be bored and could self-entertain, whether it be by cooking and preparing my own meals or doing my monthly cleaning of my room. There were several activities organised by the home in the early days which I wasn't keen to partake in if the whole group was involved. I found it very difficult being in a group full of other disabled people, due to the fact that a significant group of disabled young people brings out the patronising in local

137

communities. They see the disability first, rather than the intelligence and the power of the mind of each individual. This is why it didn't fit comfortably with me to go out in a group, whereas if I went out on my own independently, the perception of the community would be completely different. As soon as I spoke, it would be like I had no disability in the first place. Another reason for me preferring to go out independently was that people didn't know I lived with a group of other disabled youngsters. They actually thought I was living in my own flat, which was only partly true.

As my first month went on and more new residents started joining, I began to wonder why I was actually placed at Fethneys to begin with. Although it was nice to have the independence and feel like a free man when I was out and about, when I went back into the safety net of the Fethneys environment, truly speaking I didn't really feel that I had anything more to learn. I was already at an advanced stage. Were social services holding back my progression, instead of putting the necessary packages in place so that I could simply get my own accommodation? If so, why not give someone else my place, someone who actually needed to learn the skills required to move into their own home before actually doing so. When I first went to Fethneys, it felt like I was teaching skills to the other residents, almost like an ambassador for the company rather than a resident who was meant to be learning themselves.

Never be too satisfied

In 2010, when I was at Fethneys, although I didn't learn many independent skills, I would like to stress this wasn't because of Fethneys. It was because I was already beyond what they were teaching other residents. On the other hand, I spent a lot of my four years learning about myself and how I could develop my independence in a different way. I guess this was my time to really focus on what I wanted to get out of my life, and prove to myself more than anyone else what I could actually do.

In my opinion, some members of my support team often underestimated my ability. I wasn't showing much of an interest because, like I have mentioned, I was more advanced so didn't need to take an interest. But there was more to it than that. Before I carry out any task, I like to think deeply about every possible thing that could arise. I appreciate people may have taken my way of doing things for laziness. But actually, I was very, very active, putting together plans to blow people out of the water. Surprisingly enough, I found this approach very amusing and motivating, especially when all of a sudden you come to a conclusion such as 'I want to play football!' But because I gave off a lazy impression, people reacted to me as if I had had another idea which wouldn't materialise. How wrong they were!

It took one flyer that the manager had put on the residents' notice board with the information that, very soon, there would be a Saturday morning/afternoon club for wheelchair football taking place with the Brighton and Hove Albion FC in the Community team over at Portslade Community Centre. Naturally, as a sports enthusiast, my mind started powering up like Concorde getting ready for take-off. Could this be the moment to prove the doubters wrong? Time would tell. However, I was pretty sure that I was going to enjoy the feeling at the end!

I started to organise my support so that I could go to the first football practice session. It took forty-eight hours to get my support in place. For those of you who wondered why your support is always failing you, may I suggest that it is not what you do, it is how you approach the people you want to support you. For instance, if you approach care support staff in a very calm and polite manner, you are more likely to get somewhere than if you just approach them in a dictatorial way with no respect or thanks to them. For me, this was the secret behind why I got support very quickly. It helps to have respect and manners!

Part of my training from Treloar was how you manage preparation, including unpredictable circumstances. So, when it came to getting ready for my football practice, I decided to go to a car garage and see if they had any old spare tyres. Luckily on this occasion, they had plenty, so I asked, using my best respect and manners:

"Please could you very kindly chop a tyre in half so that I can use it as a bumper to push the ball along when playing football?"

This was in case I needed to bring equipment to the first practice session. They looked at me very bemused.

"What exactly do you want half a tyre for? To be frank, I'm concerned for you."

"Come on, mate. I am disabled already. What's the worst that can happen?"

"Fair enough, buddy. I will just go and dismantle the tyre for you."

"Cheers, mate. I have one more little request. Can you make some little holes, either side on top of the tyre and put some string through so it can attach onto my footplate, for security?"

"You don't want a lot, do you, my friend?"

"No, not really. Just half a tyre with holes and a bit of string would be lovely."

Twenty minutes later, I was wheeling back to Fethneys with half a tyre, holes, and a bit of blue string. Happy days! I am now fully operational, ready to kick some derriere at football! When I got back to Fethneys there was a reaction.

"Why on earth have you got an old tyre?"

"It's part of my preparations and forward planning for football."

I got the response I was hoping for.

"You've only been here a matter of week and we are already seeing skills that our other residents have never demonstrated before."

Could my actions be about to change the whole idea behind Fethneys? By this I mean, would they now incorporate the skills that I have just shown into their independence training? I always like to be involved in change, even if that wasn't at all my original intention. But it's good to see I can bring things to the table that no one has ever seen or, perhaps, thought about before. Trying to keep this up was going to be a challenge, but one I was very enthusiastic and committed to take on. For the rest of my placement, every time I organised something, I tried to use skills that I thought they would never have seen before. So, eventually they could start using them and the skill levels would be on a par with mine at least. That might be a good thing!

Another part of my preparation was to get staff to prepare me a little lunch box to take along to the practice. I was really surprised when I asked for assistance with this, as it seemed I was asking them something they are not used to doing. But to me, all I was doing was using my own initiative. Surely, as a transitional home, they were used to this? To my amazement, residents taking the initiative was something they weren't very used to. They weren't expected to initiate their requirements, which is essential to being independent, in my opinion. It is vital, and the difference between success and failure. Fethneys were obviously used to a

141

more prompting approach, rather than the fully independent approach in which the residents make the first move.

I could never have imagined from seeing a bit of paper advertising football sessions every fortnight (and making these preparations for that first training day) to go from that to, in six months, attending full training programmes with the Brighton and Hove powerchair football team every Tuesday evening at Angmering School, in order to be able to compete in the wheelchair football national league over a weekend in a destination I know well, Nottingham. To achieve this in the amount of time I had, the world really was my oyster. I'd simply blown myself out of the water, let alone my doubters!

As the power chair team was getting better, it was obvious we needed better equipment, including a wheelchair specifically designed for football. However, some of us weren't fortunate enough to have pots and pots of money. Me being me, I used my rather living-life-on-the-edge-and-taking-risks attitude. Out of the blue, I decided once again to go to a car garage and enthusiastically reveal the plan in my head that I'd been developing for months, meticulously going over it so I could get the perfect HD image absolutely spot on. I needed to explain to the mechanic exactly what I had in mind. Part of my outrageously complicated plan was to grab my spare chair and seat with the assistance of a volunteer named Alex and take it to the car garage expecting a big fat NO! But 'worth a go, as you never know'. As they say, 'if you don't ask, you don't get'. After my explanation, the mechanic grabbed some paper and a pen and started to sketch out my plan. What came next was completely unexpected and shocking, but at the same time was very loud music to not only my ears, but to my bank account too. He agreed to carry out my plan, but with the assurance that if anything went wrong, I as the individual was to blame, so he would in no circumstance take any responsibility for any accident. The fact that he carried out my outrageous plan more than showed that he too loved living life on the edge. The final result was better than that HD image I originally had. To see it on a sketch pad is one thing. When I actually saw it become a reality, that was a truly special moment, and cemented in my brain that I really could do anything I wanted to, even if it meant taking my life a bit close to the mark! In total, I saved myself £3,000. Who needs a £3,000 chariot to play football in when you can design one yourself in your mind and get someone to physically make it for free?

Now I was in possession of my free football chair, it felt the right moment to show off my creative skills, not only on the pitch but also by giving them a flavour of what I am capable of mentally. Let's go! The season was drawing closer, so I was eagerly awaiting the fixture list to see who we would be playing in our first ever wheelchair football national league appearance as a team. I didn't have to wait long for the fixtures to be revealed. Who would have thought Brighton would be playing Swindon in our first weekend of the season? But let me tell you, I could not wait to get out on that court. Exciting times! Before any of that, it was time to find myself a practice pitch somewhere near to home. Angmering School was our training base for all our sessions, as the majority of players lived in that direction, understandably, as they were also students at the school. It's not what you know, it's who you know! The day before training, I decided to go in my football chair, take my borrowed football from Albion in the Community and go to my local park for a kick around, just to test if everything was hunky-dory before going in to battle.

One thing I was particularly good at was making my support

staff go on a little jog when I completed a reverse back spin. There's nothing better than the sound of the bumper hitting the sweet spot and seeing the ball roll for miles and the support staff trying to keep up like a hedgehog keeping up with Ronaldo on the left wing. Amusing to say the least, but I was also apologetic if they weren't expecting to have a cardio workout on shift. As they say, what doesn't beat you, makes you stronger! My first independent practice session lasted for twenty minutes or so, then it was time to go for a well-deserved sit down – for the flagging support staff at least, who was probably thinking he was in need of a new body part! Great fun!

Next day on the way to training, I didn't really know what to expect, other than something completely different to the Saturday training sessions, as they were more based on having fun and the social aspect. Something was telling me this would be a completely different ball game! When we arrived, it was like my first day at school all over again. The only difference was there were far less wheelchairs, so scaled-down from Hogwarts! Although I was used to competing in sports at various levels, I felt somewhat like a lost little fish. However, once the introductions started and we played a little ice breaker, it was like I'd been doing this for years, so nothing to fear!

Given my history in sport, and the fact that I have been coached by many talented coaches before, in my head I was going over various scenarios that those coaches had previously advised me on. It was very hard at first to get out of those familiar experiences and focus on what these new coaches were advising. That being said, I quickly adjusted my thinking and matched their approach, which I found particularly interesting. A lot of their coaching was done in small groups in which they could really focus on individuals. It was very person-centred and they tried to develop each individual session by session. For me, it was a real education to see how other organisations carry out their work. It was serious, and it was also a place where we could bond, get to know each other to a level where we started to communicate outside of football practice. This ultimately led to a fantastic relationship and team ethic for our first season in the national wheelchair football league. At the end of the season, we secured our status in the Championship, which, having never competed at that level before, was quite some achievement. Well done, all, and thanks to the coaches!

Building for the future

We all have a plan to build for the future but, like a lot of people, just after leaving college you find yourself at a bit of a loose end. I had all these sports achievements and qualifications but couldn't find a job for love nor money. My relationships went from strength to strength with Brighton & Hove Albion in the Community. The more I was attending their sessions on a Tuesday evening, whether that be football or another sport, the more I grew in confidence. This was a club which gave Worthing, Brighton, and the surrounding areas the chance for people with disabilities to gain confidence in themselves through playing sport. I thought it was a brilliant service to provide our local community with options that it seemed no other community facility was offering! Albion in the Community gave disabled people confidence in themselves and a sense of belonging so that they could feel they were contributing to society, which provided a boost for mental health and well-being. There is nothing worse, speaking from experience, when it seems that we are always only asking for things and for people to assist us with our daily lives.

I think it is important that people with conditions don't let the conditions hold them back, when they are wanting passionately to make their own contributions to the community. It shouldn't be just one-way traffic, as in disabled people always take. They need opportunities and equal rights to be able to give back as much as they get.

One evening, I was coming back by train from my voluntary coaching in Worthing. A light bulb came on and I sat there thinking 'I've got all these qualifications and knowledge; how do I turn this into employment?' I had to get off the train to catch another one. Whilst I was waiting, having half an hour to kill, I started scanning through the contacts list on my phone. I came across the Albion in the Community head coach's mobile number. So, not expecting much, when he picked up, I simply said, "Hello, mate. I know this is a bit of a weird one but you don't have any jobs going, do you?"

"Funny you should say that. We are just starting a new coaching apprenticeship scheme. I can put you on the list for an interview, if you like?"

"Yes, mate. Why not?"

"OK, Adam. You're on the list. I will give you a call in a few days to give you your interview date."

My immediate reaction after the call was, 'Well, blow me down! I wasn't expecting that. How much more am I going to achieve? The world really is my oyster. You just have to have the motivation and passion to go with it, which, luckily, I have plenty of.'

The train journey home was the best journey I've had on a train in my life. Playing my favourite tunes, as well as knowing I've got an interview date to potentially start my dream job of becoming a coach. Amazing! Can't wait to tell everyone at

Fethneys and see the doubters' reactions...Interesting!

Twenty minutes later, I arrived back at Fethneys, telling everyone my news. Not surprisingly, some people were shocked. You know who I'm on about by now. Yes, that's right – the doubters. I must say it's an incredible feeling when you prove yourself, but you also know you shouldn't have to! I went to bed with an extra spring in my wheel, knowing what I had achieved that day.

I had a good night's sleep, got up bright and breezy, ready to take it easy! Only joking! This day turned out to be a life changer, as I got the all-important phone call giving me my interview dates. The phone call lasted exactly one minute.

"What is your availability for tomorrow?"

"Blimey, mate. You're eager! But thanks, because I'm a diva! Yes, I am available."

"Great. Would twelve o'clock midday be suitable for your interview?"

"Bang on. See you then, buddy. Have a good evening. Bye for now."

So, as we now have an interview date, I'd better get my wheels moving and preparations flowing, otherwise I won't be going. I got all proactive, and went down to the local information shop. This is a service for young people to help them apply for jobs, write CVs etc. On entering, I said, "I know this is a bit last minute but don't worry, I know exactly how I want to write it and what I want to write, so could you help me compose a CV, as I have an interview to get an apprenticeship in sports leadership."

"Give us half an hour, then we will be available and able to assist you with your request."

With half an hour to myself, firstly I decided to go and get a bonus chicken box from KFC, as I was Hank Marvin (starving).

Second on my list once I had gnawed my way through the bonus chicken box, was to complete my preparations. I went to Sports Direct and bought some of my own coaching equipment in case I was to need it, even though I hadn't got past the interview stage just yet. But I'm **that** confident in my interview techniques. I will get my place! After this, it was back to the information shop to complete my CV, and it turns out I was brainier than even I thought. I sat there whilst the assistant was writing, thinking to myself 'Have I really achieved all this?'

Approximately half an hour later, I had my first ever completed CV in a professional slippery fish, ready to show all my achievements and who's boss when it comes to interview technique! Not long to wait now.

Finally, tomorrow dawned. The day I had been longing for. If I could describe my feelings, I would say it was like when a kid opens a new PlayStation when they haven't had one before. To make sure I was there on time, I was two trains ahead of my actual interview time. Nothing like being prepared, I guess! After arriving two trains ahead, I had around about an hour to spare, so I decided to have a cheeky quick look around the Brighton & Hove football mega-store whilst constantly thinking 'Is this really going to be my place of work?' I found it overwhelming, to be fair. Nonetheless, I did make use of my spare hour and bought a football ticket for an upcoming league match.

Then it was time for my interview. Instead of an interview, it felt like I was taking a stadium tour, because to get to my interview room I had to take a route inside the stadium to parts where fans aren't normally allowed to go. I felt like it was a very important interview for a very important VIP. Nonetheless, I wasn't very nervous, which is unusual for me in those circumstances. I guess it helps when you already have a

148

connection with someone, especially your potential employer!

The actual interview itself was pretty much run of the mill, although there was one particular question that I found a bit personal, though I completely understood why the question was asked, and of course I had just as quick a response.

"What are you going to do at break and lunch periods if you need the loo?"

"I have in place an organisation called Access to Work, and they have provided funding for an agency to come and do my personal needs at the most convenient time for all."

Part of my preparations getting ready for my interview was to cover all bases, including personal care needs. I went down to the local Job Centre, as I knew that support staff at Fethneys wouldn't be able to support me in my workplace due to having to stay behind for other residents. So, I decided, as I said, to go to the Job Centre and booked an appointment with the Disability Adviser to ask her one specific question, which was, "Do you know of any charities or organisations that help and support people with disabilities in the workplace?"

Her response was depressingly familiar.

"I've never been asked that before."

"What! You've never been asked that before?"

"No, never."

I couldn't believe it. After we both had got over the shock, it was clear she obviously had no information on her Job Centre system, so she decided to use the world's best friend and Google it. This revealed that actually there was an organisation to support people with disabilities in the workplace, and that was Access to Work.

I now know that if you are independently minded, know what you want and how to get it, have a job offer (your dream

149

job), AND there is no support staff to hand, then Access to Work is the solution. You do have to meet the criteria and funding has to be approved, though. All went well, Access to Work gave me a great deal, and my bid for independence was secured. I was able to live and work like everyone else, even if it was only for a short period. Each year, I needed to be aware that my Access to Work funding could be stopped, as these companies for some reason frequently change the rule book and put new criteria that I may not be able to meet. Always have that in the back of your mind, so have a Plan B just in case. You never know. Luckily, during my work placement my funding was always approved. I do believe this was only because I required minimal assistance, due to the fact they were only supporting me up to an hour maximum during my break and lunch hour, supporting me with food and drink and personal care.

I am pleased to announce that the interview was a great success and they offered me a place there and then. All I had to do now was get my work uniform ordered and ready for my starting date! At the end of the interview, they said, "We think you could bring a lot to our team because of your personal experience. You already have a disability which is what we focus on in the community, so in essence you will be playing a unique role because you will be able to advise our clients and customers like no other apprentice will be able to."

A few days later, I got a nice little delivery in the shape of an official Brighton and Hove Albion uniform. Let me tell you that the sense of pride coursing through my veins was absolutely incredible and something I will never ever forget for as long as I sit on my bum. More than anything, I couldn't believe I had just got a job practically all by myself, and the funniest thing was it all started when I was sitting at Durrington train station waiting for my connection to Worthing. Funny how things turn out, isn't it? It just shows, if you have grit and determination, what is actually possible. Never say never. Having a disability is no excuse. If you have the opportunity to be part of society, you should take it! Something that really annoys me is when disabled people bang on about the fact that they don't feel they belong in society, but when you ask for information, you discover that they have been offered an opportunity, but they turned it down.

"Have you ever been offered a chance to be a part of society?

"Yes, once."

"So, what did you do?"

"I didn't take it up."

"So, what are you complaining about? You had the chance, and you blew it!"

In my view, people only have the right to moan if they are being denied because of their disability, not the fact that they have chosen to be denied. There is a fine line. If you have a disability and want to learn anything from my book, just have a little think and read over this section before approaching me. I will be on your side if you actually want to take opportunities and find that barriers are in the way due to your conditions and disabilities. I would be more than happy if people came up to me, regardless of what disability they have, and said to me, "Adam, I really want to be part of society but I'm just not sure if I have the right mindset or confidence at the moment."

I would then respond by saying, "OK, not a problem. Let's try and get to the bottom of what is stopping you from taking the wheels or steps you are wanting to take. I admit that including yourself in society when you are different can be hard to get your head around. We people with disabilities need to have a mindset that allows us to think outside the box, and do what's right for us, regardless of what we look like."

I found this out when I was between the ages of five and six, when I got my first ever set of wheels. Part of the conditions to keep the chair was a physiotherapist doing a wheelchair skills test to see how you manage your vehicle and handle reactions when in public, driving a wheelchair for the first time. I can vividly remember having that feeling of being ostracised by kids my own age. I'm guessing they didn't really know what to think when I appeared in front of them. Here was one of their friends pushing a lever which made wheels go round. What's going on? Looking back now, this is probably the reason, or one of the reasons, why I'm so outgoing and confident in my abilities. I overcame this feeling of difference and being ostracised at a very young age. You are young, and yet you do not feel a part of society. But at the same time, I was outgoing and confident. Certainly, I felt judged, I felt different. I've gone through feeling not part of society, but then also, because I am outgoing and confident, I kind of feel I should be totally honest and say I have got so used to it. I don't give a crap what people think anymore, because at the end of the day I've had some experiences that, if I wasn't disabled, I would never have had.

I think my disabilities are a positive thing, and I believe the reason why people are so quick to judge and push people aside is because they are uneducated, not because they are nasty people! I use my disability as a learning manual, not for me, but for the people that start with having a bad attitude towards me. When I have worked my magic with a bit of education, they soon change their thinking and turn their perceptions of me into a positive light! I understand not everyone has the skills to be able to do this in the same way I have managed to do. I strongly believe the reasons I can make progress with other people, apart from overcoming the negative experiences of feeling different and ostracised, is also because of the type of upbringing I've had. I have not been wrapped in cotton wool and fed with a silver spoon. I was always taught to be just myself, and was also told that people will always judge disability one way or another, and some people are naturally judgemental. It's got nothing to do with the fact of your disability. It's just the way they are.

My family circumstances gave me some opportunities to overcome barriers. For others, their circumstance will mean it will take longer for those individuals to develop the same level of confidence and attitude as me. Another reason that it will take longer may be because their parents have had bad experiences themselves, and sometimes they stop their loved ones from flying away too soon. Although I understand every parent wants what's best for their children, I believe holding people back from taking their own path is likely to have a negative outcome in their later years, which could affect their confidence and the way they engage in the community!

Is there ever a right or wrong time to leave your parents? There is no right or wrong answer to this, it is whether you are actually ready. As I sit here and write this book, I have a similar dilemma, because I am transitioning from having virtually no care hours to a live-in budget. At the moment, I've been used to my mum providing most of my support but, in my head, I am starting to prepare myself for what it will be like when I get my live-in package and my mum retires. I guess what I am trying to say, guys, is you can't rely on someone for ever. There comes a time for change. I guess for me that time is drawing closer, day-by-day, hour-by-hour. But unlike other people, I imagine, I believe I have the mental strength to be able to cope with what's coming my way! When my new enhanced budget starts, and my mum retires, she will be worrying, I am sure, about whether the new carers will be looking after me efficiently and effectively. But I would rather her worry than have to stop her life any more than she has already done to physically look after me. At least she will be able to do most, if not all of the things on her bucket list. I am confident that, over time, her worries will slowly diminish. It's been tough for me personally, because it's not so good to have a client/carer relationship instead of having a mother and son relationship. So, it will be fantastic to have my mum back.

Chapter Fourteen

Work

Access to work and work experience

With one's new job secure for at least two years, one wonders what the transition from care home to the big wide world, albeit for eight hours a day, would be like. Only time would tell. One thing I hadn't realised was that there are two six o'clocks in one day! A shock to the system. Each night, it felt like I may as well have stayed up in my chair, as by the time I landed on the bedsheets, it was time to get up again. I occasionally thought:

"If this is what the real world is all about, then forget it!"

I must say, it took me at least a month to adapt to my new responsibilities. The first challenge was to get the eight a.m. train from Worthing to Brighton, half-asleep. Nonetheless, once I was on board, I was buzzing full of energy and enthusiasm, because I knew the time had finally come for me to give back to society, which is pretty unheard of for most twenty-three-year-olds, let alone a twenty-three-year-old with a physical disability attached. I guess I was proving one thing, and that was that there **are** jobs on offer. The problem was that people my age were too lazy to get up out of bed and take the offer of employment. It seemed if I could do it, when I had no more than just a cup of tea and some cereal to have in the morning before I left, then it escapes me why people are so anti-work when they have all four functioning limbs supporting them. Unless there's a new condition that I don't know about coming into fashion called lazy-itis. If not, the mind boggles.

One thing I particularly enjoyed was early morning. Everyone would be going to work at the same time, so in a sense my disability became invisible, which is a great feeling. Not that I mind it (my disability), of course. But, at the same time, it was refreshing to not have 'labels' hanging over me.

Secondly, every day for two years, when approaching my final destination en-route to work, I was met with the amazing view of the brand spanking new Amex Stadium, home of Brighton and Hove Albion FC. As always when going into new or unfamiliar circumstances, I took my time coming down the ramp to get off the train. I also bought a bacon roll, instructed the burger van man to cut my roll into bite-sized pieces so that I could eat it and make sure all necessary gaps were filled, and in addition make sure I was alert, awake, and raring to go for my new job. There was nothing like it, that feeling of growing up before my time and eating a fat bacon roll outside my new employers. I said to the internal Adam, "Start as you mean to go on!"

After the bacon roll (luckily, I didn't lose any teeth) it was time to get rolling into the office to see what the day had in store.

Suddenly, a thought came into my head: they may be used to supporting **clients** with disabilities, but are they used to supporting **employees** with disabilities? I'm sure my outgoing relaxed persona will make it a damn sight easier for them. Or, will I have to use other tactics, in terms of not being so relaxed, in case of any hurdles in the way?

"Ready or not, here I come. No turning back!"

All this thinking what it was going to be like, it was a bit like sitting on egg shells, because I honestly didn't know what to expect. All I knew was that I would be studying sport.

While I was anxiously waiting for my mentor, Paul, to come down the stairs to meet me, you'll never guess who walked in the door. It was only the Brighton and Hove Albion manager, Gus Poyet. What an impressive guy! He may have millions of pounds but he's still rounded enough to hold the lift door open for me. What a way to start!

Paul arrived just as I got into the lift. He very generously came for a lift ride with me.

"All right, Ad? How are you feeling?"

"Better now you're here, mate, thanks."

As the lift door opened to take us into the education centre of the Amex, I could hear a voice saying,

"I know the sound of that chair!"

When I spun round, it was only my good old friend, and one of the country's best coaches, Duane. I felt immediately at ease knowing all I had to do now was to meet the other apprentices.

This is where I really fell in love with ice breaker challenges. To get to know each other, we were set a challenge. I was immediately under pressure, due to my boccia background, to be good at it. We had to throw a ball to the person opposite us whilst saying our names. For someone with cerebral palsy and co-ordination difficulties, trying to throw a ball accurately and speaking when you've got a booming spasm ripping through your body… well, it made me feel like I was one of the Transformers. I had to laugh out loud. Understandably, the others looked at me.

"What are you laughing at?"

"Myself," I replied.

"What's funny about that? There's nothing wrong."

With this one comment, I felt one of the lads already. They

157

completely ignored my Transformer impression, and, as they had said, nothing **was** wrong. In a way, it didn't feel like I was at work. It actually felt as though I was hanging around with my friends back at home. I can really reassure those of you with disabilities, there are actually some really decent people in the world, especially those who I had the opportunity to spend my first day, and also the next two years, with.

Once we had completed the ice breaker, we were divided into groups. The next task entailed supporting one another to set up a coaching session within our small groups, and we had to take it in turns to role-play taking a session. It helped us to get used to the sound of our own voices, as well as preparing for a training session. When we eventually had to go out delivering sessions to our local community for real and we had already been tasked to speak in front of all the other apprentices and coaches, I knew from the previous reactions that when I was doing my Transformer impression, I didn't have anything to worry about, even with the problems of my muscle tone and spasming while speaking. I think one of the main reasons other apprentices didn't really take notice of my muscles and spasms when speaking was due to the fact that we all had the same love for sport as each other. Nothing else, whether it be race, gender, or disability, mattered.

This didn't prevent me from feeling as though I was incapable of being a sports coach, if truth be told. I actually went to my mentor in my supervision session and said, "Paul, I don't think this coaching business is for me, you know."

What came next were the words that changed my thinking entirely.

"You are actually displaying yourself really well and putting forward lots of good advice, including advice that even I myself would not necessarily think of. And I am your mentor, so just believe in yourself, champ!"

I never knew, taking on such a job, that you would learn more about yourself than about how to teach others. Paul was pointing out that I was giving advice to clients, more advice than I myself had realised. To start with, I was not very confident. But after the pep talk from Paul, I began to enjoy what I was doing and, in the end, flourished throughout those first weeks.

The second thing I learnt about myself is that I could take guidance from those who had my best interests in mind. It actually turned out rather well. Watching another apprentice doing a presentation, I thought that I needed to change how I presented myself if I wanted to be taken seriously when delivering my sessions. So, in my next supervision I discussed with Paul the possibility of setting myself the goal of improving my presentation skills, in order to be able to deliver a better service in the local community. Paul looked a bit surprised.

"There is nothing wrong with how you are presenting yourself and delivering your work."

So, I learnt not to try and be someone else. Just be me and be happy in my own skin.

Coming back to that very first session at the Amex, it was nearing the end of the day, so, once the afternoon session had finished, I was allowed to catch the train home. It had been a true learning experience on the job. On the train, my mind was racing with reflections of how the day had panned out. The one thing I didn't realise, as it hadn't clicked at that point, was that I was following in the footsteps of the whole family and was now working. I don't think even my own family had thought this would ever be something possible. As I have said previously, when I was a small child, the whole family believed that nothing should stand in my way. But with time, they were aware of all the obstacles and of course they worried for me if things went wrong. Here's a lesson for everyone. I have shown and proved that you cannot worry about your subconscious feelings too much because what will be, will be!

When I went to Treloar, my family thought they would get the same old Adam back, one that they thought wouldn't ever be in a position to get a job. Sure, someone who had, in his own mind, ambitions, dreams, and things that he wanted to achieve. But, of course, most of the time I was boarding at school and then at college. They only saw me was when I came home, not in an environment to showcase my skills and what I'm about as an individual. Circumstances didn't allow it! I knew this, and quite often went home thinking they are going to see the same old Ad, but internally I was not that guy any more. I couldn't wait to unleash the new model Adam and wait for their surprised reaction! I guess when you don't see someone from week to week, it can be hard to believe or notice the real potential that person was showing away from his family. But my family always had trust in me and, when the time came, they were there supporting the new model Adam. From the first ever meeting when discussions took place to get my Treloar ball rolling, in reality no one knew how far the ball would go or where the ball could end up. It was just a guessing game, to begin with. How long is a bit of string? What I'm saying is really it was all up in the air, but had the potential to turn to gold. As long as I was on the podium at the end of all this, I didn't really care whether it was gold or what colour it was. All I can say is that I was ready to test myself to the max, and I knew from my first visit that that was exactly what was going to happen. In other words, it's like a testing centre for a new car, but in this case with limbs that didn't really work. As an individual, I believe I have one of the strongest mindsets of anyone in the world. You hear of these budding scientists creating new things on the moon; I was going to do the same thing but on Earth, with my body pushing to places it, or I, had never been before. And that is exactly what I achieved. Hence the term 'testing centre'!

Changing our world

I live my life by the term Mind Over Matter, because I strongly believe that the mind will do almost anything you want, as long as you don't expect things to fall in place straightaway. It's almost like you need to prepare your mind for failure, because nothing ever goes seamlessly the first time. It's how you come back from your failure that really matters. Never let success go to your head, and never let failure go to your heart. As long as we stay true to ourselves and don't try to live beyond our expectations, I see no reason why like-minded people with disabilities cannot achieve their dreams as well as anyone else! So, do me a favour, go out there, achieve the achievable. Ignore the haters, because the reason they hate is that they are obviously suffering from low self-esteem and low self-confidence, and therefore want to bring those who **are** achieving and successful down to their level.

It's the world around us that causes our disabilities, not ourselves as humans. For example, if you purchase a simple bit of equipment, such as a portable ramp, you then have the key to enter any buildings you wish, as long as you have permission to be there. People often ask me what disability I have. I have many responses, but I will give you my favourite one, and that is, "I don't have one. It's the world around me that brings to light my

161

disability, if you can call it that, with the general public."

It's a simple thing to put right. Shopkeepers can solve the problem of me gaining access to their products by purchasing a ramp or two. When they don't do that simple thing, me and others in my situation are made to feel different to the rest of the world – just because that simple bit of equipment isn't available.

Is there anyone out there who would give a helping hand in changing certain laws around accessing your local communities or communities that lie further afield, so we can all live as equals? The time is long past when people were being segregated just because of the colour of their skin. I am hellbent on not letting this happen to people with disabilities just because they need something a little bit extra. Martin Luther King would be rolling in his box if he knew people with disabilities are made to feel segregated, just because of a step lying in their way. With all the technology about nowadays, it never ceases to amaze me that I still cannot get into a night club in 2020, and you cannot blame that on the pandemic! This is as simple as people getting off their bums, helping each other out, because at the end of the day they should be thinking 'If I had a disability, I would want assistance just the same!'

Bear this in mind. Twenty-four hours after saying the above, they could walk out of their front door, be hit by a car, and then their life would unfortunately be changed for ever and, due to that life change, they would be unable to access the club that they were in just twenty-four hours earlier. I would love people's attitudes to change to a mindset whereby they never know what tomorrow will bring, and because of this they think 'I am going to help this guy to access a building while I still have the ability to do so, because tomorrow I could end up the same, if not worse, and require the same level of assistance.'

Once I have finished achieving what I want to achieve for myself, I will turn my attention to helping others to access our world for **their** convenience. I feel people need to start appreciating that some people in our society have it hard in life from the outset. It shouldn't be made harder as we get older. If anything, it should be made easier. If a little bit of plastic or metal would go some way to easing their life, then I think it's worth spending a little out of the budget and purchase equipment that will make lives that little bit easier. As Stephen Hawking would say, "It's not rocket science!"

Whilst I sit here writing this book, the whole world is going through a pandemic! Just a few years earlier, the UK government claimed to have very little money. However, I find it very strange to believe that as now, all of a sudden, they are able to dish out billions of pounds on eating-out schemes, on furlough schemes etc. However, whenever I've asked if I could please receive some more funds to make my life that little bit easier, I have categorically been denied by the local authority. They tell me this is due to the government saying that they're cutting budgets because they haven't the funds, yet they could afford to give millions of people vouchers to get half price sandwiches. It just doesn't add up! This may seem controversial, but when you are living on a budget that currently does not meet your need I think I have the right to bring up something controversial. I do think governments need to rethink how they spend their budgets and prioritise those in need over some poxy sandwiches, while lining their pockets and sitting in their gold bathtubs!

It's true what they say, money makes the world go round. I'm not disagreeing with this statement. I'm simply saying that there's a reason why authorities get given budgets, and I'm pretty sure it's not to spend on luxury biscuits and gold bath tubs. I want to give you a little insight of what it's like to be a client of an authority that do all they can to give you as little support as possible. I want to present to you the reality of what happens when you receive that lack of support. My family and I have always struggled with social services, as they try to undermine the opinions of not only myself but also my family and other people such as medical professionals, police, mental health experts – the list goes on.

I find it fascinating, as well as very frustrating, when it comes to having a personal budget review. The social service managers ask clients to log every aspect of their daily life, going into quite intimate detail, which I am hesitant to put down anyway. You can't always trust who will see the documents, regardless of whether data protection is in place or not. I still don't fully feel comfortable most of the time handing over personal and intimate information.

For this information to be considered for the review, it's the client's responsibility to complete what has been requested. You go through months of accurately detailing every aspect of your life, making it as watertight as possible so that when the allocated worker comes on their visit you can give him or her your documents, fully assured that you have done everything asked of you and more! When I completed my first ever log book so that they could see how much support I needed, I thought this was a really good tool for putting the client's opinions at the forefront of the client's wishes. It also helps the client feel very much involved and that they have a say on what happens next. How wrong could I be! As a disabled person, I have always had to put my trust in society and its systems to help me on the journey that is life, whether I wanted them on my case or not!

Sometimes, I wonder how on earth some people even get to

the stage where they ultimately have your life in their hands. What I mean by this is that I have met a lot of workers of the social services variety in whose care I would be nervous of leaving my dog. So, you can imagine how I must feel as a human, having to rely on such workers for the best thing I love to eat … and that is doughnuts. Seriously, I have had my fair share of social workers, reviews, panel disputes etc. The point I really want to emphasise is that the people who are making the decisions that could change a person's life forever have probably never worked on the front line with clients to see what actually goes on, and the impact that their vastly ridiculous decisions are having not just on clients but also their families. At this very moment, when I write this, I am contesting the lack of provision of night care!

You may recall that I said that log books were a good idea but, again, how wrong could I be. I will tell you why I have come to this conclusion. When you spend over three months getting the most up-to-date information from GPs, therapists, mental health workers etc., and you go to the trouble of making it very, very watertight and you specifically provide, in detail, information that your allocated social worker has asked for, you expect it to be read and understood. On the review date, you present all they asked for after those months of hard work, which by the way includes medication charts, waterwork charts and Christ knows whatever else. Then you wait in anticipation, only to watch your allocated worker scan through your documentation like he or she was reading the Sunday newspaper… well, it's very disheartening. Like the rest of us, most social workers just read the bits that interest them, and do not go through it with a fine-toothed comb, like you are meant to do with documents such as a care log specifically requested by the social services! It's one thing hearing that's what social workers don't do, but I am telling you, it's another thing when you see it happening live in front of you. It is very disheartening because I feel like saying, "Hoi, I have just put my whole life on a plate for you, and all you can do is go through it quicker than when you take your car through the car wash!

It then becomes doubly disheartening when you find out, weeks later, they are not going to fund the care I vitally need to save my life! Instead, they come back to me and say, "We need evidence of why you need overnight care."

"If you look at your computer information and find my latest life story, which you asked me to update, on page 20 it states exactly why I need overnight support, and also what my care needs are."

The social worker's reply you wouldn't believe. I hope you are all sitting down.

"We've not got any of your information on our system."

I found this very, very funny and actually it made me chuckle.

"Now, listen. I recently sent an email to West Sussex County Council data protection team with a freedom of information request, and what I got back was over six hundred pages worth of evidence, spanning six years. I suggest you look in your files! You are telling me you have no evidence… Do me a favour! Get an education. Or at least, a new job that doesn't involve reading complicated or not very complicated documents."

Unfortunately, this has been an ongoing battle since I became independent and it still is to this day, as I am writing! What they have to realise is that I am not just going to take their first offer and roll over and say thank you very much just for their convenience! I am going to fight for my human rights to live life just like you readers. There is no way I will settle for anything less than the best, and if it means taking my local authority to the cleaners, then that is what I shall do, if means I will be able to live my life the way I should.

Chapter Fifteen

My Flat

Set me free

In this chapter I am going to talk about what, some might consider, the impossible being made possible. In 2012, I had what I call an *Adam quiet period*. To the outside world, it might have looked as if I was being very lazy and hoping that things would just fall on a plate! But, oh, no. That was just not the case. Far from it. I was actually planning the day I would call *set me free*. As I am sure you are aware by now, before I do anything I like to go deep into thought, just like an octopus goes into hiding at the bottom of the Atlantic Ocean. If I was going to prove people wrong yet again, I knew I could not make one single error, so all my time and energy went into my thought processes. Just think of the M25 on a Monday morning. This was my head on a daily basis, weighing up pros and cons, every aspect known to man in terms of my safety and what went along with that.

One of the biggest things I was contemplating was, 'Is now the right time or shall I sit in my safety net for a while longer?'

The answer turned out to be, 'No, I will sit in my safety net for approximately a year longer.'

The reason for this delay was just to make sure that everything I had been thinking about was ironed out, before I started making loud noises to announce I was getting the ball rolling! You see, it wasn't just a case of packing a suitcase and upping sticks. This was actually the rest of my life I am talking about. Once the ball got rolling, no turning back! One wrong move could have seen my lifelong dream in tatters. So, it was worth it. All those people underestimating me! I had to be comfortable in my next movements, that's all that mattered. I didn't care if people thought I was lazy, because they would soon find out what my quiet and lazy persona was all about!

A year on, I was sitting upstairs in my room on my laptop when, all of a sudden, a lightbulb came on and indicated that the time is now!

This meant it was time to put my year's-worth of planning into action.

The following morning, that is what I did. I discussed the possibility of getting a bungalow with one of the other residents. He was absolutely buzzing for this idea. But I knew we couldn't get too excited, as we were yet to divulge our plans to the social workers. After several meetings, I can reveal to you, not all of them were polite. They did everything they could to halt our plans. Annoyingly, they won that particular battle. However, if they thought I would lie down, they clearly don't know me, as that wasn't my final option.

I began to work towards finding a suitable place of my own. What I am about to tell you next, I would love to be able to see your reactions. I GOT MY FLAT TOTALLY INDEPENDENTLY, WITHOUT A SOCIAL WORKER OR AN ADVOCATE. After visiting several accessible flats, nothing was seemingly appropriate. Then one afternoon, I decided to try a tactic called *bending the truth* so I went down to the local council housing department.

"Unfortunately, I have been given a timeline that I need to

be out of my current placement by."

"Oh, yes, and how long would that timeline be?"

I came up with a realistic and achievable time limit.

"Six months."

"Have you tried bidding on properties in the local area?"

"Yes, many times, but due to my specific needs, nothing was suitable or available."

"OK, no problem. We will see what we can do."

After approximately an hour of giving them the information they needed to get their ball rolling, it was approaching two p.m. in the afternoon. I had been down there since eleven a.m. bugging them! So, I thought I would be nice and give them a break. I left. But oh no, my day wasn't done. My next step was to find independent support workers whose job it was to help and support young people, disability or not, and help them move into their own accommodation. I would like to make the point for anyone wondering: they did actually specialise in this area specifically. So, having made contact I set up several meetings purely to guide me in case I came across anything unfamiliar. They discussed what they could offer me as a service.

One thing that they offered me was help with furnishing my entire flat, using charity services to do this. My first ever sofa was £90 from the good old British Heart Foundation. Then I managed to get some more furniture. You must be thinking 'But you haven't got a flat yet!'

Don't worry. I'm on it like a car bonnet!

I got special permission to store whatever furniture I purchased in a lock-up provided by the service supporting me until accommodation was found. After approximately three weeks of dedicated searching for stuff from the housing department, I got a call to go down for a meeting because they had some news! When I arrived, I was fully expecting for my year's-worth of planning to be turned upside-down. This taught me a valuable lesson, actually, in not to think everything was going to be a bad outcome.

"How would you feel about moving to Lancing, because we have found a purpose-built flat on the ground floor with two ceiling and track hoists installed."

"Are you joking? You're winding me up!"

"We can assure you; we are not. How would you feel about viewing it next Monday?"

"Oh, my God! This is off the hook. I can't actually believe it! Yes, please!"

On the way home, I decided to park up next to a bench and just take a minute to let this madness sink in.

'You have only just gone and got the jackpot! And the best thing is the social workers supposedly are trying to find me somewhere. I can't wait to tell them and hear their reaction when I say, "I have just found a flat and done your work for you!"'

Whilst sitting taking in my news I decided to give a cheeky phone call to my social worker at the time!

"Hi, Geoff. I have got a flat and am viewing it on Monday."

"What do you mean?"

"I mean exactly what I just said. Would you like to come and view it with me?"

"Yes. When and where?"

"Next Monday at one o'clock!"

The vibes I got back from Geoff were seemingly of disbelief. I swear he thought I was playing a prank, but he soon got the strong message. I wasn't, and actually it was reality when I turned up at the flat and sat in front of him!

It was clear from the outset there was going to be a need for adaptations. For example, to get in the front entrance to the block you had to manually open it with a key. The only way for me to be able to open it independently was first, to get permission from the association that maintains my new flat; then, to get the approval for a disabled facility grant for automatic doors to be installed with a key fob that I could press!

Crossing the threshold

The fact that when I went to view the Lancing flat there was no way I could get into it is something we didn't really cover in my independence training at college, so I guess it was a bit of a-learn-on-the-job scenario. But I can work with that. It's only a small spanner in the works. At least there's a positive. A social worker didn't cause it!

So, after doing some research and thinking back to when the extension was built on my previous family home, I knew that a solution would be possible, and all I had to work out was how to find the right key to open the door at the right time, if I wanted this small spanner to work its way loose. Time to get cracking and time to get to work. Weave some more magic. I knew I couldn't do this alone. I needed support from the housing officer who responded so amicably to my previous dilemma, so why not chance my arm and hope for the same amicable response.

The next day I decided to rock up unannounced at the housing office and explain the minor negative I had hit (not being able to get into the flat!) but also, first of all, the overwhelming positives about my viewing of the flat last Monday in the hope that she would see I am being positive. Give off good impressions about the flat. Let her see my enthusiasm and how much I wanted to sign the tenancy. By giving these impressions I was hoping her attitude would be as helpful as last time, if not more so. Off I went. When my number was called, I started by saying, "I really like the property! It suits my needs down to the ground, although I came across one or two stumbling blocks, which is the reason I am here."

"Oh, I am so glad and relieved you liked the property. What seem to be the issues we need to iron out?"

"Unfortunately, I can't open the door using a normal door key and lock so I was wondering if I could apply for a DFG (Disabled Facilities Grant) to assist me in overcoming these minor hurdles."

Surprised, she did some quick thinking.

"I work for Worthing Homes, so I will need to pass it to someone in the Lancing district office.

Pause for more thought.

"Having said that, if I send an e-mail now to Paul Cleever, who is responsible for the grants, he will undoubtedly pick it up by the end of the week."

She was still thinking.

"I have just had another thought. Give me one minute. I am just going upstairs to the office."

Approximately two minutes passed, then she came through the door.

"I have some great news. Due to your predicament, and the time-frame when you need new accommodation by, I have managed to escalate your case with my manager, which can ultimately lead to my manager speaking to Paul directly as they are in the same office. Actually, they sit next to each other."

By this point I was thinking how much better can this get? Everything seems to be falling into place just nicely. Better than how I'd planned, to be fair!

By four o'clock that afternoon, a response came from Paul via the telephone.

"As long as your Housing Association are happy for the work to be approved, we are happy to fund the grant. Your predicament (i.e., being locked out of your own flat) is exactly the situation our grants are used for. Now, it is down to your association and how much they value and rate your tenancy as to whether we can carry out the grant to its full potential."

I was crestfallen.

"Don't worry Mr Hayes, I will liaise with them on your behalf. Hopefully, this way we will have a satisfactory outcome, as it is my job to pull the strings to work in our client's favour!"

Fair enough! This situation unfortunately took two months longer than I had hoped, but nevertheless the work got approved so all was well that ended well. The job itself – by this I'm meaning the installation of the doors – took two days all in all, so basically a day for each door because they needed to make sure it met all the right regulations before giving me the nod that both doors had passed the safety requirements and were safe to operate.

I feel, although this section is a little wordy, it's important to explain, in detail, the process of what goes into getting your own property and the stumbling blocks that go with it. For those who desire their independence, hopefully, this goes some way to explaining it's not just as straightforward as picking up a set of keys and key fobs and in you go. There are actually several processes before you get to your ultimate dream of having your freedom. I am not writing this to put people off or squander anyone's dreams and ambitions. I am simply doing this to inform you to make sure that you have the right tools in your box to carry out the maintenance that's needed before the dream is complete.

After the work was complete and the doors were installed, I had never up till now felt such immense pride as I did when I got handed my brand-new key fobs for the first time. This was truly an immense occasion and a great feeling.

All I had to sort now was reading through my tenancy and making sure I understood it. This was quite an important document, and I needed to stay on the right side of the Housing Association. So far, I hadn't used the extra support from South Down Housing very much. However, if I was to make sure I understood my tenancy, I would have to draft in extra support from people specialising in housing for the disabled, and I had to know what I was letting myself in for by signing the tenancy agreement. It was good to get a third pair of evidential eyes, just in case anyone questioned whether I had done things by the book. That is not to say I didn't come across more hurdles once I had moved in, because if I said I didn't, I would be lying! More of that in a moment.

Once I had signed and sealed the tenancy, it was time to get practical, but of course I would need support with this as well. I managed to get my transition home support workers to assist me with heavy lifting and the transportation of my belongings to my flat, and then I was set up and ready to go. Given what I had managed to achieve without any training and prior knowledge, getting my belongings moved was a piece of cake, which, as you can imagine, felt very sweet. Once everything of value was transferred over to the new flat, it was then time to get my stuff, that had been stored in a lock-up, shifted over as well. Once all that was in situ, it looked more like a home rather than a show room.

One thing that was bugging me was the fact I had no carpet in my open-planned living area. So, with that in mind, I decided to use the Fethneys maintenance guy and tap into his contacts and as a result I was able to get in touch with a floor layer who specialised in laying floors for disabled people and their heavy-duty equipment. I mean, I knew by doing this I would be getting the right advice on carpets to suit my needs and the equipment I was going to need! After several conversations explaining what I ideally would want and need, I then had the power using my new key fob to come and go into my flat so that Nigel the floor layer could take some measurements and physically see what the deal was.

Once I had gained access and Nigel had taken measurements, he was then able to give me a quote, there and then, of exactly how much it was going to cost me. In my eyes, it's better to go big rather than cut corners, and in the end have to pay out more to correct the issues due to cutting the corners in the first instance. My advice to anyone wanting to achieve the ultimate prize is to budget so that you can get the best available result straightaway, rather than have to deal with issues and having to put things right further down the line just for the sake of trying to save money, because at the end of the day you will end up paying the same if not more than you would if you went big to start with.

If I was going to get Nigel to fit my carpets, I knew I had to hold off telling people that I was moving, so that by the time I divulged my news my carpets would have been laid, and I could go from A to B without falling in the middle. Although I had overcome a lot of difficult hurdles, I was under no illusions that I would undoubtedly face more when I was actually living in the flat, which very quickly came to light.

As an extra precaution and safety measure, I decided to phone up the Fire and Rescue Service to come and complete a fire safety check. I am very glad I did so, as it turned out I didn't have fireproof doors (apart from the electric doors that I had already got permission to install). As you can imagine, this was a great concern, not only to myself, but also to the inspector, knowing my circumstances of having a disability. I would potentially be at risk if we didn't resolve the situation sharply. The inspector recommended I had fire safety doors throughout the flat, apart from the bathroom door! As soon as the inspector made an application for fire doors to be installed to the Council, they immediately approved the work to be done, as you would expect.

It was also noted that I didn't have an accessible fire escape. The only fire exit had an inconvenient step that I would have had to be Superman to escape down. (Trust me. I have tried this before and got the scars to prove it.) So, bearing in mind this immediate situation, once again I had to contact Mr Cleever for a second application to install electric openings as a fire escape. Of course, yet again, he was very much on board with this and approved it immediately, insisting the work be completed within a month. This had a significant impact, as I later found out he was actually the health and safety inspector for Worthing Homes. With this being the case, my landlords had no option but to go along with the recommendations put to them. Otherwise, it was suggested I would have to find an alternative residence!

As if by magic, the next working week I got a phone call from a contractor who won the bid to carry out the work for my new fire escape.

"Could we come and have a look and investigate so we know exactly what we are working with before cracking on with the job?"

"Yes, of course. When would be convenient?"

"We could come in the next two weeks."

"I don't know if you know but there's only been given a month for the work to be completed."

"Whose bright idea was that? We are never going to achieve that to a satisfactory and legal standard."

Having never come across and dealt with these situations before, I responded by giving details of Mr Cleever to the contractors to communicate with him directly. So, that was how I left it.

The next day I got a phone call from Mr Cleever explaining he had had a very detailed conversation with the contractors and he had extended the time frame by six months. With this now being the case, I received another phone call from the contractors to re-book their visit, knowing they had a further six months, which in their eyes was a much more realistic target to be safe and legal! I then organised for them to come on their original slot of two weeks' time so that they could carry out investigations and to see what they were working with. Two weeks quickly went by. The appointment went ahead, as scheduled. The outcome?

"We have never worked on a building and structure like this before, so it is going to be interesting but don't worry, you are in safe hands."

"Phew! That's a relief!"

They discovered that behind my brickwork, I had lots of metal that had been used for installation. This would explain the reasons for my crap internet signal. At least I have learnt something new!

A week went by. I got yet another call from the contractors.

"We can start work next week."

"That's a fabulous suggestion. Probably the best I have heard this year. I will book you in. See you Monday."

The Sunday evening, I was chilling out watching nothing of interest on the box, I suddenly had a thought. Workmen and builders like their tea milky with two sugars, so I decided to go to the shop and stock up on my milk, teabags and sugar ready for the morning.

As soon as I was asleep, the birds started singing. By this I mean, it was daylight, so I only had a few hours of peace before they'd come to destroy my walls to make way for the fire door. They were due at nine o'clock, so I was up by eight o'clock ready, raring for my builders to carry out life-saving adaptations. They arrived as expected earlier than booked. Actually, the time they arrived was half-past-eight, don't-be-late. Luckily, I was feeling enthusiastic that morning, wasn't I?

The amount of equipment they had with them, it was enough to build a completely new block, let alone a small fire exit door!

"I would make you a cuppa but as you can tell, conveniently I have only one working limb!"

"It's OK, it's just like being at home. Both our wives refuse to make us tea!"

So, all in all, they had a good sense of humour, which in turn made the work go more quickly. The quicker the work, the quicker I could crack on with life. After approximately five weeks, with a week to spare, they had completed my new fire escape. All that had to be done now was another fire safety regulation check for the fire exit works to be signed off as complete, which, to everyone's delight, was done a few days afterwards. So, to go from having virtually no disabled access points to having three in the space of six months is pretty incredible, if you ask me. Bring on the next challenge!

Chapter Sixteen

Setback

Justice is served

I know I said 'Bring on the next challenge!' but sometimes we have to be careful what we wish for, as this next challenge was absolutely not part of my journey plans. It certainly tested me to the max, not only as a human but also as a member of society, and brought to light how disabled people are ultimately perceived. By this I mean, I was about to find out how professionals respond to complaints of a very serious nature from people with disabilities, and whether they would take them as seriously as they would do from able-bodied members of society. Time would tell!

Little did I know, I was about to embark on the toughest time in my life that I could have imagined!

Sometime in 2016/17, I needed to call an agency for back-up, as one of my carers went on holiday. I called an agency that I knew would send me a qualified and vetted carer. He arrived on a Wednesday evening at around about half seven or eight o'clock. I remember this well because I was actually conducting an interview for bank staff. Midway through, I got a knock at the door. It was the agency carer who had come to do my overnight shift. I can honestly say, to my eyes, the first impression was that this person was everything you would expect a good carer to be:

polite, down-to-earth, respectful, and good at the job. All seemed like any other evening, certainly nothing to cause concern, anyway.

As the evening went on, and I had finished the interview, the agency carer and I got chatting, as you do. After an hour or so, I decided enough was enough and I would hit the hay. I had already decided that, if in the future I was ever to need a carer from the agency, I would ask for this particular carer, but it was very rarely I have to use agency carers anyway. It was only because, like I said, I had a PA on holiday that I was having to use the agency. However, I'm quite funny and picky about who delivers my care, so as per usual, I decided to book the same carer from the agency for the duration of my PA's leave.

It was approaching the end of the week and we had built quite a good carer/client relationship. It was when I was told by this new carer that they weren't actually getting much work from the agency that I decided to take them onto my payroll independently. They would become one of my private PAs! Every formality in the book was taken, such as an advanced, enhanced DBS Check, formal interview, and still nothing untoward came to my attention. All the checks came back clear, just like they should be! After all the right procedures had been completed, that individual was now formally on my payroll. At least this was now saving me money. Every little helps.

It was getting towards three months of working together, on and off, and I then booked my new PA to cover another holiday, this time for a week.

"Yes, no problem. This is a good opportunity for me to earn some decent money!"

"OK, great. Glad I can help."

The week commenced, and it was just like any other week.

As something to do, I decided to go to Southampton for a day trip. The new PA came along to support me. As we arrived, the PA had a suggestion.

"Why don't we go for lunch?"

Off we went to find some food. Normally, as a rule of thumb, it is the employer's responsibility to pay for a PA's food and drink whilst on duty. But, unusually, this PA refused to allow me to pay for it. The PA would get lunch! I have had people pay for stuff on a special occasion such as birthdays and for Christmas presents, but not on what I would call a normal working day. To me, this put a niggling suspicion in my head, so, me being me, I decided to question the individual and pull them up on it.

"I just wanted to show my appreciation for you putting me on your payroll."

I took this as a fair enough reason. It is always nice when people show their appreciation.

After the food and the discussion as to why my PA paid for lunch, it was time for some retail therapy. Off we went. I bought some designer clothes and a milkshake, then some pick-and-mix sweets. I had nearly eaten half of the pick-and-mix before paying, as you do. I can't surely be the only one who does this. Maybe I am just too honest, telling you this!

It was time to catch the next train to return home. On the way home, we were twenty minutes into our journey when the PA pulled out this massive box.

"Open it."

"What is this?"

"It's for you."

My reaction was surprise and shock all rolled into one.

"Thanks again, but sorry I really cannot accept this gift, because there's a line we cannot cross!"

The PA responded in a way I have never seen or heard before.

"But I am your PA!"

For a minute or two, I sat trying to figure out whether my PA knew the difference between being a professional and being a friend. It seemed I had to explain the lines that cannot be crossed.

"If you read your contract, it explains in black and white what your responsibilities as an employee are and also what my responsibilities are as an employer. I don't see there anything about you and me being allowed to exchange gifts back and forth. Those are just the rules I am afraid. If any party breaks contract, you could lose your job, and I could lose not only a PA but also my whole care package. This is a PA/client professional contract only. So, taking this gift would be a breach of the contract, and not only that but one risk I am not willing to take. I'm sorry!"

This PA's response to my statement was, dare I say it, somewhat over the top, to say the least. I felt like I'd been punched without seeing where the punch came from. So, that evening was a bit tense. But I've had many tense evenings, especially with young carers when I tell them something they don't want to hear. As an employer, you have to do things you don't want to do. But in the long run, both parties have a better understanding once you have slept on it. After I had my evening meal, I decided to go to bed at nine p.m., which, if you know me, on a Friday evening is unheard of, considering I am a raver! However, I thought it would help the situation blow over, diffuse the tension and give time to reflect. When dawn broke, hopefully we would make a new start.

As the morning was approaching and it was quite light outside, I woke up and put the TV on to assist me in preparing my mind for the day ahead. The PA got up around nine a.m., ready for a ten a.m. start, later than usual as it was the weekend. I needed the individual's assistance with some tasks, one of which was writing in my diary to schedule a client's sports sessions. I have my own sports business, Sussex Wheel Power. If you are interested head over onto *HowIroll.com* for more information and bookings!

It seemed like a normal Saturday morning. All of a sudden, the demeanour and the behaviour of this individual changed, so fast I didn't see it coming. What happened next was the worst thing any human could impose on another human, using unimaginable physical strength. If I could give you an analogy to compare with this behaviour change and demeanour, it was like Father Christmas coming with Rudolf to deliver presents, all gentle and full of the spirit of the season, then, almost immediately, once down the chimney, transforming from all peace and tranquillity into all terror and domination. Here in my room was the Incredible Hulk! This terror, this domination over me was the reality, much to my overwhelming disbelief. No more a PA, someone had arrived in my flat to terrify me. This time is the only time in my life, still to this day, that I have felt totally vulnerable. This, evidently, is why medical professionals call us disabled people vulnerable.

During this very terrifying and quite unbelievable situation, all of the gift- and present- buying was starting to make sense: I was about to become a victim of assault. During the ordeal, everything such as the niceties, over-friendliness, the enthusiasm and willingness to work extra, it all came together like glue in the end. The individual was just waiting for the right moment when I would be, and he knew I would be, at my most vulnerable: on my bed!

However, let me tell you something. There is a bodily

response mechanism to overwhelming danger that we call fight or flight mode. This is the body's way of reacting to trauma, either physical or mental. In this instance, physical flight and physical fight were not possible. But mental fight would be an option, even if it was delayed. All I kept thinking throughout was 'Wait until I get into my wheelchair. Then I will regain the power like a million volts going through a railway track.'

After what we now know as The Assault and My Ordeal, my brain began to generate power. I could actually feel the power gradually getting stronger and stronger throughout my bones, to the point where my heart was having palpitations. It was as though my impulsive and reactive thinking was about to take off. But I knew I had to wheel very carefully if I was to get the right support in a couple of hours. So, this is what I did. I acted normally, as if nothing had happened. It was just a normal run-of-the-mill Saturday afternoon.

"Now, can you hoist me into my chair?"

"Yes, of course. No problem."

The person did what I asked.

"Are you OK?"

"Yes, why wouldn't I be? Absolutely on top of the world. Thanks to you."

I then instructed the care worker to go and do the washing up, as there was quite a lot to do. In the meantime, whilst this individual was carrying out the tasks, I sat in my chair and thought.

What the f*** has just happened to me?"

I was left with two options: (1) deal with it myself and see a lot of people I love and care about go to prison for a long time (because of what my family would do in retaliation), or (2) outsmart this person mentally, now I had regained my power, and send a message: you may have got the better of me physically but I am not to be underestimated mentally.

I decided to go with the option that would give me the most power, option two. I wheeled out of my bedroom. Seeing my PA obviously made me jump if you consider what had just happened, but I ignored this startle reflex.

"I am just going to phone someone. I will be back in five minutes!"

Outside my flat, I began to phone someone who I knew would stay calm under such extreme circumstances. That person was one of my other carers, Gumbo, who I have known and trusted with my life for ten years. As I was explaining things, unfortunately the signal dropped out on my phone. I knew that I had to be quiet so that my attacker wouldn't suspect my plans. If that happened, my power would have very quickly diminished and I probably wouldn't be writing this now! Although out of immediate danger, I still had to be mentally switched on and aware, because walls have ears. Luckily, as I was about to escape through the entrance to my block of flats, someone else was coming through the door. She'd caught my conversation on my mobile and, to my surprise, said, "Did I hear you right? You've just been assaulted?"

"Yes, it's not something I go around bragging about. Yes, I have just had the worst ordeal anyone can go through and been assaulted."

"Do you want me to call the police?"

"Yes! What do you think!"

The police were called. Once they arrived (they had first gone to the wrong address), I can honestly tell you I felt like **I** was the criminal. It was seeing two police cars, each with two policeman arriving at the same time, so in total there were four police officers coming towards me, each one with their handcuffs unclipped and ready for use. The first thing they requested was for me to hand over my flat keys.

"Don't worry. You're not the one in trouble! We are doing this as part of a safe-guarding procedure."

I would like to reassure you; no handcuffs were used on me! It was then decided that two officers would stay with me, and two officers would use my keys and go round the back to give the individual the nicest and biggest shock and surprise of his life. My attacker had no idea what I had been doing, until two uniformed officers with their hand cuffs unclipped were unlocking the door. They walked in to arrest my assailant for an horrific assault on a vulnerable adult! This is the last actual sighting I had of my attacker, as he was marched to the police car. My internal reaction to that sight was that this is what you get for messing with a physically vulnerable but sharp-as-a-tack adult.

But it doesn't end there. In fact, we are just getting started. In this whole episode, you will find out the harsh reality of what victims of violent, sexual assault like myself have to go through to get justice served on disgusting criminals. It started that morning, when I re-entered my flat and saw it turned into a crime scene just like in Silent Witness. They were taking swabs to trace DNA, photographing from every angle possible. They even were taking away my favourite Chelsea duvet set for evidence. But needs must. Now is the start of their building up unquestionable evidence to put before a court.

To be continued.

Knowledge is power

Unfortunately, part of that crucial evidence was to examine me as an individual, which let me tell you was categorically the worst experience of my whole thirty years as a citizen on this planet. Just when I thought the whole thing was coming to an end, and was heading back towards my flat feeling as though I had just been run over by an emotional train, just when I needed time and space to gather my thoughts, just when I had started to commend myself for saving thousands of vulnerable people from having to go through the same ordeals, or worse, that I had gone through, and just when I was about to press my key fob to open my flat door, a rather hench-looking copper came towards me.

"I am so sorry, Mr Hayes; you are still not allowed to gain entry, due to the fact we are continuing to gather evidence to support your already unbreakable case against the perpetrator and to get you the right outcome and the justice you surely deserve At this point I regret to have to inform you that a key part of the concrete evidence is in fact yourself. We need to get you to our local examining centre, otherwise known as the Sark Centre."

Total disbelief. Even more, it felt like bullet holes thrust through my chest. After all I had been through these last hours, I have now got to be examined! This was becoming intolerably harrowing.

Before I could even get to the examining centre through all the mayhem, everyone seemed to have forgotten about my physical disability and how the hell I was going to get there. Local enquiries were being made to get me a taxi but, as per usual, local taxi firms were refusing to send their vehicles, as my chair was apparently too big and they claimed the weight of my chair would damage their ramp. Just what you need when shit is already hitting the fan! Whilst everyone was fighting over who would NOT take me to the examining centre, I was sitting in the corner thinking to myself, 'I really cannot be dealing with this. I might just drop the charge.'

On the other hand, if I were to drop the charge, I would not just be putting myself at immediate risk, I would also be doing my disability community a disservice by releasing an animal back into the wild. I found the mental strength deep within my soul to plough on through and do whatever it takes to get justice for myself, my family, and my community. Thankfully, those thoughts were enough to persuade me not to drop charges. But I am not going to lie, the pain I felt was worse than when my hip dislocated permanently and I can assure you that was really painful. I'm not normally one for rolling around in pain, but I was certainly doing more than rolling!

It's certainly times like this when you really realise what true love and commitment is all about. People couldn't have been more supportive than they were at this tragic time. So, for that, I would like to thank those who showed the true love and respect they had towards me. I would like to say sorry if I snapped like an alligator at times. That was purely my emotions speaking. I was having an out-of-body experience. At one point, I am sure I even saw the pearly gates, my emotions being so raw. It was almost like I was getting a dagger through my chest cavity every time I spoke!

I thought that if I could cope with rolling in physical pain, I could surely cope with the intense mental pain I was currently feeling, even if it was getting worse every second. Surely this is worth getting justice for thousands of potential adult and child vulnerable victims! At the same time, I felt as though my body was going into sleep mode. I had lost touch with my surroundings, and I only realised they were still trying to organise transport for my visit to the devil, aka the examining centre, when my brother turned up and said, "Sod this. I will take you in my car."

Hearing the voice of that person I trusted with my life shook me out of that deep sleep I was hiding in.

"OK, I am safe now."

Hearing my brother's voice, I began to let my guard down. I allowed my brother to pick me up and put me into his car. Once I was in the car, he shut the passenger door, and during the moments between him putting my manual wheelchair in the boot and getting into the driver's seat, the car fell completely silent. I was on my own island. Sadly, it was too brief to comprehend things and gather my thoughts!

Instead of giving me quiet and enough time to gather my thoughts, the sound of the engine starting meant it was about to take me to be examined by the forensic nurses. Thankfully, my brother had some dance tunes to at least give me some respite for the journey. I began to dream that I was actually on the way to the airport to go off to Ibiza, rather than to be put through a dreadful, brutal physical examination. When I say 'brutal', I mean mentally, not physically. Physically they were as gentle and considerate as could be, but to my mind it was a completely different kettle of fish! However, during the journey, it suddenly occurred to me that maybe all this commotion has done my future mental ability the world of good, because, weirdly, I began to feel the worst had happened to me already, so whatever comes next will be like water off a duck's back. After this, no matter how hard people try, they will never be able to hurt me again.

Although I was having a brief there's-light-at-the-end-of-the-tunnel-moment, I also had to deal with the reality of being examined, which was just round the corner, as I could see sign posts for Crawley. Once we arrived in the car park, all of a sudden, some unwanted thoughts cropped up. Would I lose my lifelong dream? Had I lost my chance to live an independent life and had I lost the flat I had fought so hard for? Was all lost in a single day to a severe safeguarding concern?

These thoughts got stronger and stronger, to the point when I actually thought it was going to happen, as a specially trained social worker walked into the waiting room. I immediately wanted to ask some questions regarding what had happened and the consequences it would have.

"Now you're here, does this mean the end of my dream? Will they take my flat away?"

"No, not at all. However, we will look at installing various safety measure to prevent that happening in the future."

I was about to take a sigh of relief, knowing my flat was safe when a forensic nurse was stood at the door.

"We are ready now. Do you want to come through?"

At this point, it was actually lucky I couldn't walk, otherwise the doubt was so strong that I would have walked to the sign that said Way Out. But my brother had control of the handle bar of my wheelchair.

During the examination, although it was very traumatic to my mind, I had to keep thinking that they are just doing their job, nothing else. Likewise, I am sure they were also thinking what a shame it was that that they were actually seeing clients on an hourly and daily basis for the same reason as me! What I am trying to get across to you is that the feeling was 99% mutual, in the sense that as much as I didn't want to be there, they didn't want to be having to examine me. But I guess someone had to be able to catch dirty criminals and put them away.

Altogether, the examination lasted fifteen to twenty minutes. After that, I went back into the car to return home, by which point the uniformed police returned my keys to allow me to re-enter my property at approximately half past one to two o'clock in the morning. Finally, time to relax as much as possible. I did chuckle to myself, though, when I saw my cup of tea and medication for that day still sitting in the exact spot it was left in.

The following morning, I felt a great deal of numbness and wasn't very forthcoming when it came to communicating with people. This carried on for the majority of the day, so I thought maybe it was over-tiredness and went to bed, only to find out I was exactly the same the next day, though this time, with only a day's break, I got a phone call from the CID department at Littlehampton requesting me to come and give yet another statement. I could only assume it was going to strengthen an already locked-down case even further. In the back of my mind, I knew also I was dealing with detective inspectors who are specially trained to look out for signs of doubt in both parties. Yet, I can tell you that with my eyes closed, back to front, upside down, telling the scenario word for word, ten times over, if needed, I was supremely confident no doubt would be found!

As the time for my interview came closer, I found I was terrifyingly reliving every angle and position in my head, just to make sure I hadn't missed anything that could be crucial evidence for the justice system. Suddenly there was a copper-like knock on the door that sent me six foot in the air. When the door was opened, I was pleasantly surprised to see the detective, who would be in charge of my case as it went forward, was actually already known to my family, due to being the ex-bobby on the beat round my local area, back in the day. On this realisation, a cell in my brain sparked and gave me the strength I really needed to push as hard as I could to get this animal brought before the courts. I now had to give another lengthy statement, in more detail than I had anticipated, which as you can imagine left my brain in dire straits. But, as I previously mentioned, this pain and terror are worth going through, especially knowing the end result would be golden for me and slop for my assailant.

After giving my lengthy statement, it was then revealed I would have to go and do a video evidence interview for court and jury purposes. This would show the court and jury what an impact this whole situation was having on my life. In my opinion, this was the most important part of the whole process. The videoed interview would be the key to justice and would assist the jury in deciding whether the verdict was guilty or not guilty.

Obviously, travel was involved. It wasn't just round the corner. We had an idiot of a taxi driver asking us what we were doing and why we were going to the police station. My response is simply not repeatable for the book. But you can imagine. Put it this way, it wasn't whispering sweet nothings in his ear. All that I could put it down to was the fact that his life must be extraordinarily boring, to feel he could ask this of me. I still had time on this journey to get my mind back to the purpose – to get back to business and get justice.

While I was waiting to go in to the recording studio, it felt as though I was waiting in a call-up room ready to play a boccia match. I was as focussed as an athlete before a race or a match. The hard work had been done previously. Now it was time for battle. Leave nothing out there.

The best way to describe the whole scenario? It was like being on an episode of Piers Morgan's *Life Stories*. It was just a room with magnolia walls, two chairs – one of which was empty as I had my own wheelchair – just two people, one being the detective, the other being me (aka the victim), and a camera in the left-hand corner of the room. The camera, plus microphone, would pick up not only the interview but also the sound and honesty in my voice and all the different tones of emotions and facial expressions, which is the whole point of a video evidence interview. It makes sure that all the specialists, detectives, judge and jury along with barristers, can identify if the victim is being sincere and honest. It works both ways because, just imagine if the perpetrator was innocent, you are effectively changing their lives as well. The court participants need to perform their crucial part and the videos meant they had to be as sure as humanly possible that they are serving animals like my assailant the right kind of justice. I would just like to say, this doesn't mean the justice system were starting to doubt my evidence. It just strengthens my case further, whilst giving the perpetrator a fair representation – innocent until proven guilty, and all that.

The interview was very emotional, raw and intense but, like I said, I left nothing out there. After a few days I felt better, as I knew I had given all the evidence, despite how very graphic it was, to the best of my ability, which is all you can do. Stay true to yourself but, most importantly, state the facts. I guess now it was a waiting game for the CPS to decide whether there was enough evidence to take it to the crown court!

About six months went by. It was a Tuesday night, and I was on the bus to work when I got a phone call from the detective saying the CPS had decided to charge the individual on all counts, so all that was left to do now was compile all the evidence ready for court.

I would just like to inform you, readers, from me first reporting the incident to the individual going to prison took about two years. Please don't be fooled at how quickly I've given you the information. Two years of my life. The process was longer due to the fact that the original courtroom scheduled to take my case at the last minute was found to be inaccessible for my wheelchair, so we had to wait for an alternative courtroom at a different court to become available. You would think it wouldn't take long, but unfortunately it does when there are thousands of animals in the wild that shouldn't be taking up court time!

During this period when I was playing the waiting game, I'm not ashamed to say I did have some suicidal thoughts and made one attempt. This is the reality when, for a while, everything is happening at a pace where you don't even have time to blink, and then it changes, and nothing happens for months and months.

Naturally, things started moving eventually and then the reality of my court appearance loomed large in my mind, which became overloaded and I couldn't cope. I get exactly what people mean when they say people must be at their absolute wits' end to have such thoughts and attempt to carry out such drastic measures, because I once was there.

You can't hide forever

In order to get justice, like anything in life, it takes time. Unfortunately, in this case, time can be a killer, more mentally than physically. I had all these terrifying thoughts and feelings, pulsating, twenty-four hours a day, seven days a week, three hundred and sixty-five days a year, for two years. It was like October 31st Halloween most nights. The devil would come calling and try and manipulate Little Adam into causing myself potentially life-threatening damage. This devastated my soul, I'm sad to say. Never underestimate people, or think they are being ridiculous or trying to seek attention when they say they can hear voices in their head. Speaking from experience, when the devil was speaking to me, it was really, really convincing, to the point that it led to me carrying out my suicide attempt. Trust me when I say that your brain gets severely traumatised when you have been damaged. Please support those in need and give them a shoulder to lean on. Don't assume anything and impose your own opinions on damaged people, when you don't really know or have any understanding of what people may be going through!

For many months, I kept a lot of what was going on bottled up because I didn't want to give anyone the bullet holes or nightmares I was going through. It felt right at the time to keep it to myself. But if I had to go back in time, I would do things a lot, lot differently. Certainly, one thing I would do is shout from the rooftops exactly what was going on in me at the time, and make sure it was heard by those outside of family with no emotional connections with me. Looking back, maybe my suicide attempt was probably the moment, for once, I sought support because I really needed it in my life. This was my saving grace. People who didn't know me that well suggested seeking help was totally out of character. I was acting like almost a totally different person.

"Adam's in serious trouble emotionally to be on the edge of life the way he is."

The suicide attempt shook me to my core. Even back during my drinking days, I would never have considered anything like that, and I was numb to pain back then. I can assure you I was close to being sectioned; it was that bad!

On the way home from my walk that night, I sunk into what I consider a strange state of mind. I was giving myself a ten-minute breather. Ten minutes was the difference between me being on this earth to write this book and not! At the end of that ten minutes, I took myself through my door, and went straight to bed to safeguard myself, because in bed I can't move. Once everything was quiet, and my carer was in the next room, I managed to somehow smash the devil in the face, hard enough not to wake up till the next morning. This allowed me a safe space to finally reach out for the support I needed before I lost complete control, which would then end my life.

I decided to call the Samaritans. If I am honest, a lot of people slate them, and say they are no good and they don't work. If they don't work and they are no good, then someone please tell me why I spent the next six or seven hours on the phone to them. The phone call finished at four a.m., as I fell asleep on the phone! Maybe those individuals that slate this life-saving service haven't admitted to themselves that they actually have a problem and need help. If you are worried about being judged in your crisis, these people are specially trained to deal with any critical crisis in people's lives. They are not there to judge you. They are not there to air an opinion. They are simply there to be someone to listen and then to speak to you impartially and on the level. They are volunteers. That volunteer I spoke to on the phone was the first step to what I now see as my recovery, as that volunteer was able to give me further advice on who to contact, providing me with email addresses and phone numbers to services that are specially trained to deal with my specific crisis! So, for those who slate the Samaritans and think they are no good, I suggest you think again because they are life-savers when you are at your most vulnerable times. What most people do not think about is this: what you have been dealing with in your crisis, you are now off-loading to the volunteer working for the Samaritans. After the call, they have to deal with the emotions you have just passed on. These are special people if they can do that job. I can tell you that for free! I certainly wouldn't be able to do what they do, that's for sure! After the lengthy conversation, I managed to let my damaged soul have some respite.

When I woke up, I felt that now maybe I would be able to

rationalise about my damaged life, recall that phone call and put more safety measures in place – things that arose from that conversation that I could put into action. I seem to remember waking up at eleven a.m. which was unusual for me. The biggest thing I noticed was that it was like the feeling you get when you have just woken up from an operation and you don't quite know where you are, disorientated. My brain was put into recovery mode as a result of my obviously much-needed deep sleep.

I struggled during the day to make sense of what was going on around me. My concentration span was low. I couldn't focus on anything for more than twenty minutes, half an hour, as anxiety and impulsive behaviour reappeared. It was almost as if I was wheeling on internal beds of nails; one wrong move would have been the end of it. I was petrified to do the simplest things. Once upon a time, any one of these simple things I would have done with no problem whatsoever. However, I could only deal with what was in my head. Unfortunately, those things were very much unwanted, and caused me to struggle at times even to speak, as I was so afraid of sparking my emotions! Imagine you are at a firework display and you can't even hold a sparkler because in order to activate even a sparkler, you have to light it. This is how my emotions were every day for two years!

As days went by and the investigation was hotting up, I was being called by the police to give evidence from every angle and make statements at all different levels in preparation for the court appearance. The biggest and most challenging one was of course the video evidence and my emotions were starting to get sparked and my unwanted friend, the DEVIL, reappeared. When I was providing various statements, it was like being shot without a gun involved. Every question was a successful shot and then after the question, the devil would say, "I enjoy seeing you like this.

That's why my best friend (i.e. my assailant) pleaded not guilty: to land us even deeper into turmoil by dragging you and your family through the courts. So much better than pleading guilty, don't you think?"

The devil was also saying, "We know what we've done is wrong, but we think it's funny not to admit the truth."

After one particular police interview, what started with one devil became a field full of devils. So, to deal with that and to safeguard myself, I actually admitted on camera what was going on in my head at the time, and that I needed a break from the questioning. I took a break for five minutes, admittedly the anticipation of waiting and knowing there would be more questions lobbed at me was quite simply unbearable, so the break in actual fact made no difference. I decided to crack on with the interview and deal with the consequences afterwards. I was in the interview for approximately an hour, excluding the break. Unfortunately, that hour long meeting stayed with me for months. I didn't really know where to turn next. I also found it incredibly hard knowing I had to rely on people not just for my physical being but also now my mental being. Effectively, for several months, maybe a year, I was totally dependent on people to help me through life. It's bad enough knowing you can't do stuff physically, let alone having your mental independence ripped from you as well. This left me feeling little more than an inconvenience to society and not my normal self, and I was someone who normally would have a positive effect on the community. I did wonder whether I had done something seriously wrong to someone to deserve this amount of trauma.

After the video evidence interview at the police station, I decided to bite the bullet and ring Victim Support for further emotional assistance. Of course, yet again, there was a waiting list longer than my arm, because unfortunately there's lots of filthy animals committing assaults and consequently also people suffering the same or similar traumas to mine! After a three-month wait, I finally got a text from my Victim Support caseworker. Our first meeting didn't happen because we were in the same place but couldn't find each other. I thought to myself 'I can do without playing hide and seek with all what's going on.' In all honesty, it did cross my mind whether to cancel the support altogether, as unfortunately it took three attempts for us to meet each other. As you can imagine, the Adam you all knew before, the confident Adam, had totally disappeared. Anyone's first impressions of the unwanted new Adam were... well, unrecognisable. I was sad. I was angry. The way I reacted to the smallest things was like a volcano erupting in a desert. Luckily, my Victim Support worker was trained to deal with all these different emotions. By the end of the first meeting, she managed to get me to shed a tear and quite honestly, I can't remember the last time I did that. She obviously unwrapped a nerve that was severely tangled, almost like a cassette when the tape deck chews the tape.

Week by week, it was almost as if she emotionally took me apart and rebuilt me layer by layer. I have to say, throughout the two years I had support, I didn't feel alone inside any more, because I felt someone found the loose wire that had come adrift from my emotional circuit board. I am making it sound easy, but in actual fact whilst the rebuilding process was happening, my emotions got worse and I really knew who my true friends are, as unfortunately due to my emotional state back then I said some things that people didn't like! However, for those who stuck by me whilst I was swimming the Thames, when at times I thought it would never end, thank you very much for all your support; it means a lot. You know who you are.

A couple of weeks to six months into Victim Support, thankfully she took the reins when it came to speaking to the police and detectives, and when organising me for the day of the court appearance.

Judgement day

The organisation for the court appearance wasn't great and my time to shine didn't go without mishaps. All I needed after everything! It was decided that the case would be held at one of my local Crown Courts. With only a month to go before my appearance, my support worker and I got a phone call from the witness care team and the police.

"Sadly, the court for your case isn't wheelchair accessible."

I can't repeat the thoughts running through my head so I will leave that to your imagination! Due to the demand in court cases, my appearance was postponed while we waited for an accessible courtroom to become available. Then we got another phone call which I can honestly say was not music to my ears. The only accessible court was in Portsmouth, Hampshire. After all the to-ing and fro-ing and a bit of bobbing and weaving, a court date was finally sealed. All I had to deal with now was my anxiety and those emotions building back up. My appearance in court!

However, whilst we were waiting for judgement day to arrive, my support worker was very, very clever in preparing me. She focussed on my thoughts and feelings about this first ever Crown Court appearance so that the rebuilding process wouldn't get smashed apart on judgement day. The putting-into-place of building blocks and repairing of bullet holes was postponed till after the court appearance, because there was bound to be some more emotional turmoil to come once my attendance at the Crown Court started!

It was now a week before the trial. I would like to say that when you are working with support workers who specialise in cases in which their clients have been violated, it is really important to be as honest as you can and leave no stone unturned. If you don't do this, the end result will be like when you shake a bottle of Coke and then open the lid. Explosion! And Crown Court is not a place where you want to be exploding or doing anything to put yourself into *bad shoes*. Therefore, I took my own advice and admitted to my support worker, "I am not sure if I can go through with this. Can we just bin the case and drop the charges, please? As my head will need examining by a neuro-surgeon otherwise!"

As a positive consequence of what I had said, my sessions with my support worker were doubled, so we could really focus on my anxiety and avoid outbursts in the courtroom. We focussed on seeing if we could put a lid on it, just for a day. Our aims were to get the right justice and to keep me wearing *good shoes*.

The way my support worker managed my emotions (one wrong move and boom I would go off like a cannon!) was absolutely extraordinary. It takes a special person to do that. Before the court proceedings started, my support worker revealed that she had noticed a slight change for the better in my personality. What was once an out-of-control volcano was now on the verge of being controlled.

"You may not realise it, Adam, but you have done a lot of the work yourself, without me needing to guide you on the right path. If you can do this, your court appearance will be absolutely fine, and I am behind you 100% of the way, right to the end!"

It was the court appearance in two days, so I had two

sessions back-to-back to go through any final thoughts and see if I remembered anything else crucial towards the case. But as I've mentioned, I had been living with this and replaying this in my mind for a year now so there was nothing new. It was just as fresh as a newly baked cookie. In fact, I couldn't wait to offload this rubbish, because it was like being constipated mentally.

"Time to go now. Enough is enough."

When I got into bed, two nights before court, it was just myself and my headphones, sitting directly in front of a sea of night and sleep and my music. I was deeply in tune with my music, basically on another planet. All of a sudden, I looked up, saw the moon shining quite bright and then out of nowhere came this outline of what looked like a young girl. I can only think this could have been one of my old school friends who sadly passed away before we were about to start college together. I assumed an angel was looking down on me, and this gave me the confidence boost I clearly needed. Weirdly, on the way home the next evening I reprised this image when I selected a certain tune on my phone. This time it was a male outline that appeared. I believe these images were a tell-tale sign that people were watching over me. It gave me the belief I would be all right. It was approximately ten o'clock in the evening so thought I had better head home as I would be up early for judgement day!

I believe I only got two hours sleep as my mind was racing like Lewis Hamilton at the British Grand Prix. As soon as I fell asleep, it seemed it was time to get up and face the biggest day of my thirty years of existence. It was seven a.m., as far as I can remember. The taxi to take me to court was due at eight. I remember this well as my brother came with me, and it was the longest journey of my life, knowing what scum was at the other end.

We finally arrived. I have never felt nerves like it. It almost felt like *I* was on trial, and at any moment the paparazzi would come and start flashing their cameras. I remember wheeling into the court reception, looking up to the ceiling.

"Wow! This really is Game On! Let's have it!"

Once we had gone through the security scanner, we were met by the witness care team, and we were taken to the witness waiting room for yet another anxious wait. I wasn't alone, as I had some members of my family, my support worker from Victim Support and, unfortunately, several witnesses for other court cases which could only mean one thing: these crimes never stop.

I suppose we were waiting around about twenty-five minutes to half an hour, when my barrister came to meet me and informed me that I would take the oath and that he would ask me if I am telling the truth. Let me just mention he wasn't saying this because he didn't believe me. It is a mere formality and routine. He also informed me that he had been sent down from London, especially to support and deal with my case. This was the kind of case he specialised in, which I've got to say put me a little at ease, but not much.

He then decided to lift the mood. He would show me his Lego cufflinks and tell me that his wig was over a hundred years old and had been passed down from generations in his family!

"Mr Hayes, I will see you in court in a moment."

There was a short delay due to the fact they had let my assailant sit in view of people walking the corridors. They removed him from my sight, as I was going in the lift to the courtroom. A bit close for comfort, don't you think?

The moment I set wheels in the courtroom, the smell of authority and importance was amazing. To watch it, in a drama on TV, is one thing. To experience it in real life is another thing altogether. Just, wow! You couldn't second guess it, I'm telling you.

It was the procedure of court for all parties involved, apart from the jury members, to introduce themselves and say what their role is. Then the room fell silent. There was a knock at the door behind where the judge was going to be sitting. Everyone stood, then the judge entered the room to take up his or her position. Only when you see the red gown do you know this is the real thing. To start with, as mentioned, my barrister formally asked me was I telling the truth. Then I had to take an oath. Only then did I begin to feel I personally had it in me to take my stand on my own behalf in front of the most influential people in our society: judges and lawyers and jurors.

If I were to describe the interrogation, I would say it was almost like playing my very first game of badminton, because as quickly as they would ask and fire questions at me, I would fire back just as quickly with a response. My responses were short and sweet. That way, the defence barrister couldn't play those normal tricks and make me out to be a liar.

Some of the questions they asked were the same old questions I had answered again and again, but they were asked in a different way. So, advice to anyone, make sure you listen to the question, the way it has been phrased, and not what you expected to hear. And be sure not to jump the gun too quickly. Let them finish the question, then answer it. If you agree with the cross-examiner, you say: "I totally agree." But, if you do not agree, say, "I totally disagree; it is just not the case." You and I have to remember that they are doing a job, defending their clients, so they will try any trick in the book, including working you up so much you end up in tears, like in my case. But when it happens, do not worry. It doesn't mean, just because they made you emotional, that you will not now be believed. If anything, it went in my favour, because it showed the jury how traumatic it was for me.

I am not ashamed to say I needed to have a break, because the questioning was relentless and the exact way they put things is really tough because they say things, like, "You wanted this to happen. You gave permission for this, didn't you?"

As long as you stick to the facts and the truth, you will be fine. In total, I think I was in court for around two hours being cross-examined. There is no better feeling when you hear the judge say to you, "Mr Hayes, would you like another break?"

Or when the judge says to the assailant's barrister, "Change your line of questioning. Enough is enough."

It was when I heard this, I began to believe that I had sealed the assailant's fate. I was achieving what I thought was totally impossible; I had beaten off the assailant's barrister and I knew the judge was on my side. Just to let you know, I declined the judge's offer of a second break.

"Let's just crack on!"

Most people think you go to court just the one time and then it is all over. That's the way it looks on TV. In reality, when you are building up to a court case, a lot of work from all different kinds of specialisms goes on behind the scenes. For example, the witness care team are a vital part of the court process. They are responsible for making sure that for the duration of the witness's time spent in court, it runs as smoothly as possible. Then you have something called a pre-trial visit. This means before the real McCoy, the witness gets a chance to go and look around the court, so that when you get there for judgement day it's not so alien. If you are anything like me, you do your own preparation, and part of that requires role play!

It's important to mention that those involved, including the court officers, take every precaution possible to ensure safety, dignity, and respect for us, the general public. In my case, this involved screening me off from my assailant, so I couldn't see my assailant and my assailant couldn't see me. I was offered to sit outside the actual courtroom in the video evidence room to carry out the cross-questioning. But for me personally, I wanted to be in the courtroom so the jury could see me face to face and not just on screen. The reason I did this is because when you are trying to get justice, it's all about having a big impact and so they can see live exactly how much talking about your ordeal is distressing you. These things are what the jury look for when deliberating someone's guilty or not-guilty plea. When you are being cross-examined, the jury are watching your facial expressions very carefully as well as listening to your tone of voice when you answer.

Perhaps what people don't realise is the fact that barristers are actually trained to manipulate and catch you out when you are least expecting it. So, my advice would be to prepare diligently and do your homework, because if you think you can walk or wheel into a courtroom and take on some of the most professional lawyers this country has to offer, then think again. It is anything but a breeze! Only speak when you are asked to speak and don't speak out of turn, unless you are requesting a break or time out. However harrowing this may sound, there have to be no chinks in your armour. Any small inconsistencies in your account will be pounced upon. Anything not quite accurate will give an opportunity for the defence lawyer to make your case appear weak. Keep on track and you will be absolutely fine. Trust in those who have trained for years to get all sorts of people from every walk or wheel of life the right justice. Justice then will ultimately be served if it is meant to be!

Whatever people say about all of this, never be worried, even if at the end of the day facing Crown Court is undoubtedly one of the biggest challenges we face. Just remember this, during my time at Crown Court, all sorts of thoughts and scenarios, wondering what opinions other people might have of me, were running through my head and yes, like I said before, there were times when I wanted to pass the gold medal to the assailant, as I really felt the pressure and found it unbelievably soul-destroying and very demoralising. But I knew my version of events was too strong to let the assailant take gold, so I just pushed on through my mental lactic acid. Just as when you are running a marathon, you can see the finishing line but you just want to give up. However, those who are very mentally strong, somehow, find it deep within themselves to push on for victory. And thankfully that is exactly what I did.

The assailant got his just desserts and was found guilty, and that meant a lifetime criminal record. There was a three-year custodial sentence, and a three-year stretch out on licence. This meant if the assailant were to enter the out of bounds area specified during this three-year period, that would mean going straight back to prison to serve the rest of the three years behind walls!

It may seem weird to the reader, but the actual assault itself has become somewhat a distant memory. My focus through this whole process was actually not on myself. It was on those who haven't got a voice and find it difficult to express how they feel, especially when they are around predators such as my assailant. So, hopefully, I have saved thousands, if not tens of thousands of lives being destroyed and waiting lists getting longer because my assailant is no longer allowed to work as a carer or with vulnerable children or adults ever, ever again. Let's face it, who would want to employ someone with a CV like that. I wouldn't call it winning the lottery or the golden ticket to a better life, would you?

I was only needed in court for one day. That is how strong the evidence was against the assailant. After my evidence had been given, I started to wonder what the assailant could possibly give in defence, other than it was consensual. Then I thought, no, too much evidence to be denied. Absolutely smashed out of the park. That person has no legs to stand on.

Once the case was brought to its conclusion, I could turn my attention to what all this had done to me. I was reassured by my Victim Support worker, whose job it is, unfortunately, to deal with these cases on a daily basis, that this is a process that comes naturally to any victim. I found this very comforting. It started at the end in the courtroom. I began to relax so much that I was having a good old look at the architecture and how amazing the old parts of the building looked. That didn't take away from the fact that waiting for the assailant to give the very non-existent evidence and then waiting for the sentencing to be passed was mind-numbingly boring, almost like waiting for a train that has derailed but, in reality, has disappeared, never to be found again. To be honest with you all, I also felt a little excited waiting for the sentencing, knowing the absolute terror to that criminal those three years would mean. Prisoners do not like assailants such as this one. My physical ordeal lasted approximately an hour, but that was nothing compared to what this person will be facing from wakeup time to lights out. Every single second, minute, hour, day, this will go on continuously throughout his three years in Her Majesty's Prison. Just to put things in perspective, a reliable source informed me that one day in prison is like six months every day for the length of the sentence!

It was a Thursday and I had my phone on loud, which I very rarely do, only for special occasions, trust me. This was special because it was D-Day, the day of sentencing. My phone could ring at any moment telling me the outcome. It was around two p.m. and I was actually in a coaching session when my phone rang with no caller ID coming up, so I thought I'd better take this. I was so glad I did, as it was the inspector in charge of the case letting me know that my assailant had been handed a six-year sentence altogether, three years in custody and three years out on licence. This wasn't the only sentence, because he would be put on the Register of Sex Offenders for life, and his care worker career was absolutely 100% over. As stated before, thousands if not tens of thousands of lives were now safe and secure, and they could sleep at night knowing such a predator was behind walls and even on release they could be sure at least one predator would never be allowed in sneezing distance of them. If sexual predators try breaking the conditions set by their licence, then it's back to sleeping on marble beds for the rest of their sentence, if not the rest of their days – it depends how much they like prison life!

The day after sentencing, I allowed myself a proud moment because, even though this had been a horrific period for my family and me, I felt like a true lifesaver.

Finally, assailant, are you happy with your achievement? You thought you could get the better of a so-called vulnerable adult. Jesus, I bet your mum is so very proud of you and all that you have achieved. As a result of your vile and inexplicable behaviour you have actually made me stronger, so thank you very much. If you think your prison experience was bad, and this sentence was long, then the next time will be a thousand times worse. Mark my words.

If there is a next time, the victim's witness statement to the judge prior to sentencing will have a lot more damning evidence. For those of you who aren't familiar with judges' witness statements, this is a special statement that you write as a victim only to the judge about how the case has affected you, not only physically but mentally, and again you need to be as honest and open with no hidden secrets or niggles. This statement helps the judge decide what sentencing to pass based on how traumatised victims have been left.

It's now been a few years since all the drama. I am pleased to announce all is going well. I still have good and bad days, but I have got the tools to know exactly what to do when my bad days crop up. If I ever walked into my assailant, I would have no problem. I might even shake their hand and say, "I feel sorry for you, mate. You must have had issues back then. But we both know you dealt with them in the wrong way, which ultimately landed you in the naughty boy corner, and if I could ask you one thing it would be: did you underestimate me, even if it was just for one second?"

So, I hope I don't leave you guys needing counselling for the rest of your days. I hope you have got an insight into what it is like when you go through something horrific and where you have to go and what you have to face to get justice in this country… I'm gone. What's next?

A new me

I always knew that after everything that happened and what I went through, I would need to make certain adjustments to my emotional switchboard, because unfortunately a specific section of my switchboard got water-logged due to the horrific trauma I went through at the time! (See page 57 for my switchboard analogy!) So now it was time to replace those traumatised elements and put in lovely new shiny ones. I wanted to get back to what I do best, and that is helping my community out wherever possible and using my skills and knowledge to better the lives of those around me with the same needs or similar!

I feel now is the right time to explain whilst all this commotion was going on, I was doing my best to live as normal a life as possible. I was still running my business and attending my local community college at the time of the court case! That was five years ago. Both Little Adam and Big Adam have changed and now I am, hopefully, a stronger and brighter Adam. I'm very aware changes didn't happen and won't happen overnight or the next day. This could actually take until I reach my forties, but you who know me personally have started to see glimpses of the new circuits trying to spark into life. I really am trying to use all the tools and advice given over the years by experts to change my outlook from what was once in a dark graveyard into a scene like you would see at Walt Disney World in Orlando, Florida. I just can't put a time frame on how long it will take for that bit of circuit board to recover and for the wires to be put back where they should never have left! I now know who my true friends are, because no matter how full of strife my circumstances have been over the last few years you are still here, so thank you. Hopefully, some of you readers will stand by me as you will be eager to find out the results of the newly wired switchboard, because if my plans are anything to go by, it is going to be one hell of a ride forward. So, strap in. Get ready for an almighty party! Look out, Ibiza!

Chapter Seventeen

Trains

Nan and Grandad

From the moment I was brought into this world, on 8th November 1990, I was handed very gently, as I was so fragile it was like handling a china doll, to two legends that would turn out to be my biggest inspirations and heroes: my nan, Joyce, and my grandad, Roy. As a child, I often would visit their house in Goring. I always looked forward to spending time there, learning from their life experience and listening to their stories. I was told about my grandad's time in the army, especially about the boxing career he had there. He always told me he received more punches than he gave.

"But, grandad, your nose still looks as good as new!"

"No, I don't know what you are looking at, Sharky."

He thought I had teeth like a shark, because every time he gave me something sweet, especially chocolate, I would take it so quickly I would accidentally bite his fingers.

"Jesus Christ, you've got teeth like a shark!"

So, the nickname Sharky lived on. I have many memories but two in particular. I always knew when it was a Saturday, as my nan and grandad had a tradition where they would buy a Chinese takeaway on a Saturday night. It would be exactly the same order without fail. Secondly, I always knew when it was a

Sunday, as my nan cooked a roast dinner, in my opinion, better than my local Toby Carvery, and fit for a king. The best bit about my Sunday visit was knowing that I would get a supreme cooked roast, including the most stunning-looking giant sized Yorkshire puddings, and in the winter months, Nan's banging stew and dumplings – those dumplings were each the size of a tea plate.

Whenever I visited them, I knew it would be time for education. Grandad would take me out, in the manual wheelchair that I had back then, for long walks, chatting for hours about history and in particular how certain buildings around my local town were built. One time, he started giving me facts about a building we were passing and revealed he helped to build it. It was an old factory, and Grandad was responsible for planning its structure. He took immense pride in observing that, thankfully, the building was still standing.

"I must have done something right, or it wouldn't have survived so many years and in all different kinds of weather."

Another thing we used to talk about and have a common interest in was boxing. Without fail, Grandad used to inform me every weekend on a Saturday that he had got up with the birds to watch the boxing highlights on Channel 5. He had two favourite boxers, number one: Mohammed Ali, number two: I can't remember his name now. Their photos were always on the mantlepiece or in the chest that was positioned in the lounge with not a speck of dust on it, that's for sure. In actual fact, my nan and grandad were that house-proud, most mornings, as part of my grandad's daily routine, he would get on his hands and knees and polish the kitchen floor so it would shine like glass. I think the only day he put polishing the floor off were the days I was due to come round, because of the mud that would be on my wheels. But you can bet your bottom dollar, as soon as I left, out came the polish.

If ever I needed advice or someone to talk to, I knew Nan and Grandad were both all ears. If ever I was to take any advice, it was always them I would take advice from. It could be about anything, from how to deal with society to how it was back in their day. To this day, and certainly in today's society, I find their advice is still top notch. I am proud to say, when I tell someone the actions I am going to take – for example, when dealing with certain groups of professionals – it is actually my Nan and Grandad speaking. I am simply the physical embodiment of what they taught me.

One thing is for sure, Nan and Grandad believed in being firm but fair. They didn't mince their words.

"Today's society is like a holiday camp compared with when we were brought up!"

I loved to listen to their opinions and always took note of what they were saying. Depending on the circumstances I was faced with, I adapted their advice to suit myself. You understand why I call them the Two Legends, more often than not. Hence, I am forthright just like them, and frequently send the person I am dealing with away with their tail between their legs. And yes, I would like to reassure you I always aim to be firm but fair and to be honest without any holding back. But not rude or offensive!

I particularly enjoyed it when Grandad strongly advised me that, due to my disability, if anyone tried to make me wait to go to the loo, this is what I should do.

"This is very bad for your body, so I recommend you soil yourself, as it would be their fault for making you wait and, therefore, they would have to take the consequences: the nice job of cleaning up! Never let people tell you when and where you need the toilet, as no one should ever be put in that situation.

Wherever you be, let your wee and poo go free!"

One day we were out on one of Grandad's long walks, when I realised that I had forgotten to bring a vital bit of my equipment, so my grandad found the closest thing that resembled what I had forgotten. He picked up a discarded Coke bottle.

"Here, let's just use this."

"Grandad, you will need to use your engineering skills and make the hole bigger!"

Conveniently, he had something sharp enough in his pocket and chopped the end off of the Coke bottle. It wasn't the most comfortable of experiences, but as the saying goes, when you need to go, you need to go! I guess that taught me to always double-check I have got the right stuff before I leave the house. Grandad carefully left the full bottle where he found it.

"At least someone will get a fresh and free pint tonight when they come on their nightly walk to the beach! It will be too dark to notice exactly what it is!"

A snapshot of my grandad's sense of humour. Our walks always used to end with a trip to our favourite bakery in Goring, where we would buy a selection of doughnuts and cream cake as evidence to Nan that we had had a great time.

As I was developing into a young boy, it became evident to my grandparents that I was fearful of trains. At the bottom of their garden was an allotment, and behind that was a busy train track. Every other second, I would have to brace myself for a train to come flying past. This would make me jump due to my startle reflex. That is something that most people with cerebral palsy have to cope with. Everyone has it, but with cerebral palsy this is heightened, for some reason. I gave myself the nickname *Jumping Jack*. In order to crack this fear, one day when I was visiting my nana and grandad's, they had come up with a cunning plan. It involved another of Grandad's long walks.

"We are going on a surprise walk today!"

"Are we? Where are we going?"

"It's a surprise. Wait and see!"

Off we went. Of course, I kept asking "Where? Where?" as I don't really like it when I don't know what's going on. I kept seeing sign-posts for one of our local stations. It suddenly dawned on me where we were going.

"Oh, no!"

What made it worse I could hear the buzzing of a live railway track, as it was quiet.

"Don't panic! It'll be OK. We are just going to sit on the platform for a while so you can get used to the fact trains will come and go at various different speeds. I will sit you against the wall so you are nowhere near the yellow line, and you will be perfectly safe."

So, he sat on the bench next to me and started chatting and telling me the difference between an electric train and the old steam trains, which to be honest I found fascinating. Educational, you see! Part way through, my grandad suddenly paused midway through his sentence.

"Grandad, why have you stopped talking?"

"Shush! Listen!"

"Listen? To what?"

"It's getting louder. This train is not scheduled to stop here, so brace yourself!"

And before I could look up, there was a train halfway through the station. Must have been going around sixty miles per hour, as I could feel the wind and the G-force of the train whizzing through the station. After a moment or two, the train had gone. I looked at my grandad as if to say, what the hell was

217

that? All was quiet again.

"See! it's not that bad, is it?"

"Well, *I* can't think of anything worse!"

"No, no, no! If you think like that, you're never going to get over this, so I think we'll come back next week. Persistence is the key, my son!"

The type of train I am talking about here are the ones with the guards' van and not quite electric, more diesel. After about eight trips to various stations, I was finally over my long-term fear of trains. Each station visit, each passing week, I was able to sit there doing something different, reading a magazine, eating crisps, until I hardly took any notice of trains coming and going at various speeds. My clever Nan and Grandad!

I wondered what clever ideas they've got up their sleeve next. After returning to my nan and grandad's house, my grandad wanted to test if our several visits to the station were working, so he decided to stick me at the bottom of the garden facing the train track to see whether my reactions would be any different. The bad news was I didn't have long to find out and I could always tell the speed of the train before I actually saw anything. So, I was always bracing myself whatever the speed. It was just a case of would I be able to brace and get my body under control by the time I saw the train. The answer was unfortunately no – well, no for the first couple of weeks. But by the time we had hit the end of the month, my reactions to the trains were no different from my reactions when cars were passing by on the roads. By then, I had trained my brain into thinking that trains are just cars that travel in straight lines and can't bump into each other. I'm glad to say nowadays I very rarely jump at the sight or sound of a train.

All of that training is thanks to my nan and grandad, I can now use trains as a public service without having any concerns and without my previous fears. So, thank you Nan and Grandad. Miss you always. Lots of love, Sharky.

With Nan and Grandad, I often had a range of conversations from serious to comical, from boxing to Formula One racing, from Formula One racing to the ups and downs of everyday life. One of the most special conversations I remember having was when my nan and grandad told me about the moment they held me in their arms for the very first time. They told me I weighed the same as a bag of sugar and that I was able to fit in the palm of a single hand, no problem at all. They were fascinated that I looked like a china doll, which made me laugh profusely, especially when my grandad used to say, "So, what the hell happened? Because you certainly don't look like that now!"

I really enjoyed my nan and grandad's company. When I used to go round, it got me away from the hustle and bustle of everyday life. I thought of it as a transition into peace and tranquillity and, as I've said before, a time for education.

I remember staying for a weekend with them, which meant I got to see my grandad's routine in action. It consisted of getting up between four and five every morning, heading downstairs and having a wash in the kitchen sink, getting on his bike, heading to the sea front where he would search for useful stuff, all different kinds of seashells, pebbles, and general hidden treasures of the local area.

Then he would take his bike to the local Tesco, pick up his daily paper and a few bits of shopping, and head home by approximately nine a.m. Once he was in the door, he would change into what he called his comfies, and then just potter around till my nan got up. If I wasn't staying, that would include polishing the kitchen floor. After his daily chores, he would sit in his usual chair in the front room, open the TV guide, see what was on the box and settle down and crack open a beer or two in his favourite Thomas the Tank Engine cup. Whenever I stayed with Nan and Grandad, I always went back a stronger person. I would put into practice their wise words, without worrying about what other people thought about it. I knew if I followed Nan and Grandad's advice and examples, it would be the right approach, because it was based on old school values. I believe this is one of the reasons why, when my brother was looking after me, he did such an outstanding job. He too was following their example.

Nan and Grandad were the kind of legends that, if I was in the wrong, they would tell me in no uncertain terms, and help me to see how to get back on the right path and deal with things in the right way. In other words, if I was in the wrong, they wouldn't stick up for me just because I was their grandson. They would actually agree with the other party! Then they would say to me, "Lesson learnt. Now you know not to make that mistake again!"

Every single day, to me, my nan and grandad are still alive inside me. If I am, for one reason or another, facing a difficult task or set of circumstances, I think back to all the advice they gave me and then think to myself how would they have dealt with the circumstances which I am faced with. A recent case in point is my fighting the social services for a live-in care package. They would say, "Be completely honest, firm but fair. Put across exactly what you need, not what you want. If the process becomes long and a bit like a game, go along with it. If you are true to yourself and if it is meant to be, you will win in the end!"

My nan and grandad will always be alive inside me for as long as I'm on this Earth, and their wise words will still have a major impact on the years ahead. So, thank you, Nan and Grandad, sleep tight and save me a space for when we meet again!

Train of thought

I would like to give you as my loyal readers an insight into how I deal with my emotions in my own way. When I was studying on a counselling course at Northbrook college in my local area, we covered a certain topic called Passing Thought. The best way for me to describe this is by employing an analogy from my time with my nan and grandad. Imagine you are sitting on a train station platform. Now, imagine every passing train is a thought, coming in and out of your head. The trains **arriving at the station** are good thoughts. The trains **leaving the station** are bad thoughts and the trains that don't stop are just **passing thoughts,** and not really going to stick around. These passing thoughts can include bad thoughts, but the train doesn't stop so as soon as the train has passed those bad thoughts are no longer in my life. Another way of putting it is that the trains (or the thoughts) that stop in the station are for me the ones I can hold onto because they are good thoughts; and the ones leaving the station are thoughts to be considered or that I can revisit if I need to! Or to put it yet another way: what you need to focus on are the trains passing one another, because this is exactly how the mind works when it comes to thought processes. The reason I've decided to put this in the book is because I get a lot of people asking me how I stay so calm, and this is one technique I use – thoughts that come, thoughts that wait for me to process, thoughts that I am glad to send on their way! A key thing when we are talking about passing thoughts is how we can approach anxiety. Remember, anxiety is just another thought and, sooner or later, it will pass just like the train. We have to remember, especially in these times when we are all on an uncertain journey, keep strong, be decisive, and always remember no one is on their own!

As I'm giving tips of how to manage things, another one I use is called **stream thinking**. By this I mean, if you are lucky enough to have the sea or a river or a lake on your doorstep, imagine your thoughts are the water moving downstream. If the current of the water is calm, this means for that moment life is all good, but if the waves are rough, this **can** mean exactly the same. Our lives have rough patches. It's just natural. Just think the water currents are your thoughts calmly coming and going without resistance. Just let it flow, good or bad. When it gets rough, just ride it out, because it will calm eventually.

I hope this section helps at least some of you. Never be worried about being you, because no one knows us better than ourselves. I know sometimes people say that they do know you or what you are going through, but I believe it is only that they are trying to be supportive and considerate. The reality is that it is us and only us that know exactly what we are going through. The people around are just our leaning posts and support, if needed! To simplify things, we are in control of our own destiny, and we should only take advice if it is good advice and it will benefit us and make things better in our lives. For me, I only let the people who I trust in, if I am having a hard time. I don't take advice just to be kind to that person. What I do say is, "Thanks for the advice but it is not appropriate at this moment in time. If a situation arises and your advice comes in handy, I will use it, so I will keep it on my shelf just in case."

Chapter Eighteen

Q&A

Finally, a Q&A. Fire away

<u>Did you benefit from attending a school and college catering for young people with disabilities?</u>

I guess when I was introduced to the world of disability, aged twelve years, it taught me a valuable lesson: to go into every situation, good or bad, with an open mind and no pre-judgements. In my opinion, you should only judge a person or circumstances when you know the full details. When I first made my journey to Treloar School, on the way we had to pick up some students who were starting the same day as me. Up and until this point, as you already know, I thought I was the only one in the area, besides my cousin and those who also went to the special unit I did at my mainstream school, with a disability. I was then surprised, even shocked, to see that, compared to the disabilities that were in front of my eyes, I was leaning towards able-bodied because I had significantly better speech and was fortunate enough to be able to communicate to a high level. When I encountered people who either had a speech impairment or found it hard to communicate, my first reaction was to face this challenge head-on and see if I could find alternative ways of communicating for both those with the impairments and those without, just like I would back at home. I wanted to bring some of my experience,

223

gained from being surrounded by able-bodied people, to begin to not only find ways to communicate, but also change in a positive way the perceptions of others. I am always thinking long-term.

Where did you get your inspiration for thinking long-term from?
My inspiration for thinking long term and sticking to plans meticulously came from watching other people's plans fail at the early stages. I put myself in their shoes and their situation and started thinking, 'if I was in their place, what would I do differently to find a good conclusion'. I will give you an example from resolving disputes. I look at disputes from two different angles, one for people I do not know, and the other for people I know well. Either way, I do not tend to have the capability to stand there for hours on end and argue the toss. With people I do not know, my approach is to stand back, observe the situation, then when I think it's appropriate, give my point of view, as a calming influence, rather than turning it into a fuelled fire fest. I sit on the outside rather than take centre stage. The second angle, with people I know well, is that I just tell them this is not helping anyone, bang their heads together, and say get on with it.

That's your way of tackling disputes. But how did you find the motivation for planning your own life, especially when things were not working out so well?
I am a very driven person. I will drive through brick walls and shout very loudly until I get the outcome I was imagining at the start. I came to this by realising one day, after I had made several mistakes in one week, that, upon reflection, I needed to change the way I approached situations. I changed my thinking from short-term to long-term, which naturally gave me more breathing space. That meant I had a longer period of time, especially when

significant problem areas came up. My mistake in the past had been to put too much pressure on myself by not setting myself a more realistic time frame. When I was contemplating getting to the flat that I am in now, I said to the council, "I have only six months and then I have to get out."

The timeline of six months wasn't a pressure placed upon me, but it was for the council. This approach helps me in a range of situations. Take, for example, in my DJ career. I was advised that when you are in a club and you think you are having a bad set, it is not what happens at the start that matters, it's whether you have a strong finish. At the end of the day, that's what clubbers will remember. Another analogy is boxing. You could be losing a twelve-round fight, but if you knock your opponent out in the eleventh round, you have still won.

<u>This book is about growing up with a disability. Do you see any advantage in having a disability?</u>
Nowadays, yes, I do feel there is an advantage to having a disability, and I don't mean being able to park on double yellow lines or using a free disabled toilet with a key. I mean, the advantage has to do with being able to educate and help people to change the way they perceive people with disabilities. I don't like the word disability. I prefer *different ability*. I have a short phrase to describe this: **my disability is my ability**. I just have different abilities to other people.

There are other advantages. The most striking advantage is that having a disability from an early age means you become very, very good at problem-solving, probably at a much younger age than children who take their abilities for granted. There's no better advantage than knowing that you are able to change things for the better for yourself, and subsequently for those with different abilities coming along behind you. I like to show others that there are things they can do to feel more on a par with their school friends at the start, rather than, as in my situation, having to change some things in order to feel on a par and included. You may recall a while back in my book that I went to play football with some friends and got hit in the face as a consequence. You may have thought to yourself that I did this because I felt left out, but actually this wasn't the case – it's natural for me to include myself, whether or not they want to include me. The real reason I wanted to go and play football was to highlight in a physical sense to my school there was an inclusion problem. The best way possible to highlight such issues is to physically demonstrate them. So, that is exactly what I did.

Do you ever feel that able-bodied people don't make the most of their abilities?

I think they think that they are untouchable. However, sadly, every day is a risk, and unfortunately many people either don't realise it or don't take it on board. It only hits home if they have a bad accident or abuse their bodies which can either disable or kill them. Of course, make the most of your abilities. That's not so much the problem, it's that they take their abilities for granted.

What I have to say to the able-bodied is that it is the same for you as it is for me. Just as you should make the most of your abilities, I have to make the most of my abilities, but my abilities are different from yours. In that sense, we are not different.

I do feel I have a responsibility to the able-bodied community. As I have said, I am a very driven person and part of my drive is to support local educational authorities and their schools to improve disability awareness, and make sure the youngsters of today have a good attitude towards those of us who

226

are physically challenged. As well as all this, I like to make sure that youngsters of today make the most of their abilities and not take them for granted. I have many tricks up my sleeve to make sure they rethink things before taking ability for granted. One example was when I was asked to lead an assembly for approximately one-hundred and fifty to two hundred pupils. I began by plunging the room into complete darkness by turning off the lights and requested for the whole hall to stand up.

"Would you all please stand up."

I left it for around thirty seconds and then spookily said:

"I can't do that."

I left it for another thirty seconds before asking them to sit down. I asked for the light to be switched on!

"Why do you think I did that?"

A hand went up.

"Yes?"

"To make us think how lucky we are and not to take things in our lives for granted. And be thankful for what we have."

Another reason why I engineered this scenario was because kids of today are very influenced by their peers. For example, if someone has somehow got hold of illegal drugs, then they are easily led into handing out these drugs like sweets whilst forgetting the dangers that could happen to their health as a result of taking illegal substances. So, in this episode, it was to make them think twice about possibly sacrificing their ability just because they were thinking they wanted to be cool in front of their friends. The ease with which they were once able to do things could be stripped away within seconds, so, yes, that was another reason behind it.

Another thing I did was to ask the assembly, "If a miracle happened and I was suddenly able to walk, would someone instruct me in how walking is done?

227

I would never do this with young children, but these were sixteen-year-olds. I was impressed by one of the answers:

"I wouldn't tell you to go left and right, left and right. Certain muscles would have to adapt and get stronger and then get used to the way of walking."

That gave me just the right lead-in to wheelchair sport. They would need to adjust to wheelchair control, just the same, or they would never get anywhere.

"You then would have to think it through. You see, adaptations have to be made."

What in your opinion is the best way to relate equal opportunities to people with different abilities?

I am going to say something controversial. The reason there seems to be a lack of respect and, worse, a rise in hate crimes towards those who are physically challenged, has to do with the perception that those with physical challenges get a superior amount of privileges. Take travel discounts, for example, such as a free bus pass and a third off train travel, when the rest of the population have to pay full whack. In my opinion that isn't equal rights. On the other side of the coin, there is still a need to make every public space accessible to those with physical and mental challenges. It is essential that everyone has access to all places in their local communities or, indeed, world-wide. Any block to access we must challenge immediately, and not give in until it is removed. Only then will we see the gap between the able bodied and the physically and mentally challenged in society close. That is what equal opportunities is all about, not financial privileges.

You mentioned hate crime. How can society best tackle that?

As I have already said, I think the reason for the hate crime is not because of our disability. It is because of what we get because we have a disability. It is all about being treated equally. My view on hate crime is not necessarily to do with the fact that we have a disability, it is actually to do with the fact that disabled people get more support than the average person. For example, free disabled parking with blue badges. A third of train travel off, and free bus passes. The list goes on. However, I think if those advantages were taken away and the community had no gap to be bridged, then hate crime, like I say, in my opinion, would significantly decrease, as there would be no favouritism and we would be a much more equal society. I would agree with these reductions in disabled privilege only if I saw a change in terms of step free access where ever you were in the world!

If I were asked to speak at a hate crime group and the people attending were attending the group because they had committed, or someone thought they had committed, a hate crime, my first mission would be to understand directly from the offenders their definitions of a hate crime, and whether they actually realised they were committing a crime. Then I would suggest a little activity, where they would work one-on-one with each other, with scenarios on paper and they would have to work out whether the scenario on that paper is a hate crime or not. So, hopefully by the end of the workshop, they would be more educated and mindful of their actions before potentially committing another crime.

Some people who have been reading your book may suffer from depression, anxiety or lack of confidence. Do you have suggestions for them on how to develop a positive attitude?
Thank you for the question. I must stress this is a very close subject to my heart and indeed one that I am very happy and proud to suffer from. When I say 'suffer' I don't mean curl up in

the corner with a cup of Horlicks and cry about it. I face issues and challenging times head-on, with a practical and, as far as possible, a calm approach, so I can rationalise what the problem really is and then build it up piece by piece until I have the perfect mirror image of the problem in my head. That is just a bit of an insight on how I deal with problems and issues, no matter how big or small.

Something very important to say is NEVER STOP BEING YOU. If you suffer from depression and anxiety, just roll with it. Let your emotions flow like a river. Don't be put off by other people's opinions. Best of all, don't put on a mask for people, just because they would like you to be a certain way or a certain member of society. If they can't take you as yourself, in my opinion, this may have a negative impact and make your mental health worse because they are not allowing you to be natural.

A massive part of my life has been counselling. If it wasn't for having counselling since the age of twelve, I can honestly tell you my path would almost certainly have been completely different to the one I am on now. For example, when I took to excessive drinking, I used to use it as a coping mechanism almost to the point where I did myself permanent liver damage. Or, for another example, my anger outbursts which, looking back on it, were actually part and parcel of my depression and anxiety, could have potentially landed me in Her Majesty's Care Home (aka Prison), disabled or not, if I had not had counselling. Therefore, I am **advising** you, (**not telling** you), if you suffer or feel that you have depression, please don't suffer in silence. Just get the help on offer, whether it be having counselling for the rest of your days or simply talking to someone you one hundred per cent trust with your life. For me, this particular approach works. And I am proud to say still does to this day. Don't be put off by a society that is generally very opinionated. Just do what feels good and best for you.

You seem to me someone who likes a challenge. What will be your next challenge?

The word 'challenge' changed for me when I went through my assault. The word that I prefer to use is actually 'adventure', because once you've been through an horrific ordeal, as I went through, life is no longer a challenge. Having had the experience of attending a court of law, if I had to do it again I would do it without a second thought. It is no longer a challenge for me. So, when you ask me what's my next challenge, I find that difficult to answer. Whereas if you said to me, what's your next 'adventure', you would have to put tiger tape around my mouth to shut me up. My next adventures are to:

(1) go to university to study to be an occupational therapist and have the satisfaction that the people I support are having a fulfilled life as part of my professional and working influence.

(2) turn my book into either a fictional film or a documentary film - either of these options I would be comfortable with. But if you asked me what my preferred choice would be, it would be to make a documentary so you can physically see the adventures I was taken on!

(3) possibly adventure and challenge rolled into one, is once I've got so-called celebrity status as a result of my film or documentary, to go into *I'm a Celebrity* to conquer the jungle and all that comes with it. Snakes and all.

More to the point, I want to prove that absolutely anything is possible. Whether you are the best walker on Earth or the best on Earth at taking on physical challenges, anything is possible. The worst thing someone could say to me, with the amount of drive and determination I have, is **no**. I would do anything in my power and use every last ounce of my being to say **yes, I've done it**. Let's move on to the next adventure. I really and truly believe that the only person responsible for limiting what we do is ourselves, no one else!

<u>Do you celebrate Nation Cerebral Palsy Day?</u>
I have cerebral palsy. But I do not see that as a blueprint for me or defining me as a person. I see it just as something that happened. Fortunately, or unfortunately, it happened to be me. One of my bugbears is having a specific day dedicated to those with cerebral palsy or, for that matter, people with poor mental health. In my opinion, having a disability is neither the reason for any success I have had throughout my life, nor the reason for any success I will continue to have from now to the end of my days. My achievements are due to me as a person, not my disability or physical challenges. Actually, there is nothing to celebrate. But if you were to have a day called Achievement for Everyone Day, then we can all celebrate our achievements both individually and collectively as a country. I see no need for stereotyping an achievement! The only thing I can celebrate as a result of both me as a person and my disability is the fact that I have just won my case to have live-in care full-time!

To be continued…Here's to the next thirty years!

Notes dictated to Greg Gardner, January to December 2020